PLAINS FOLK II

PLAINS FOLK II

The Romance of the Landscape

BY JIM HOY AND TOM ISERN

Drawings by Don Johnson

UNIVERSITY OF OKLAHOMA PRESS

NORMAN AND LONDON

BY JIM HOY
(with John Somer) *The Language Experience* (New York, 1974)
The Cattle Guard: Its History and Lore (Lawrence, 1982)
Cassoday, Cow Capital of Kansas (El Dorado, Kansas, 1984)
(with Tom Isern) *Plains Folk: A Commonplace of the Great Plains* (Norman, 1987)
(with Tom Isern) *Plains Folk II: The Romance of the Landscape* (Norman, 1990)

BY TOM ISERN
Custom Combining on the Great Plains: A History (Norman, 1982)
(with Jim Hoy) *Plains Folk: A Commonplace of the Great Plains* (Norman, 1987)
(with Jim Hoy) *Plains Folk II: The Romance of the Landscape* (Norman, 1990)

Library of Congress Cataloging-in-Publication Data
(Revised for vol. 2.)

Hoy, James F.
  Plains folk.

  Contents: [1] A commonplace of the Great Plains—
2. The romance of the landscape.
    1. Great Plains—Social life and customs.   2. Farm
life—Great Plains.   3. Folklore—Great Plains.
I. Isern, Thomas D. (Thomas Dean), 1952–
II. Title.
F595.2.H68   1987   978   87–5082
ISBN 0–8061–2064–9 (v. 1 : alk. paper)
ISBN 0–8061–2272–2 (v. 2 : alk. paper)

The paper in this book meets the guidelines for permanence and durability of the Committee on Production Guidelines for Book Longevity of the Council on Library Resources, Inc. ∞

Contents

The Great Plains

Great Plains Boundary • • • • •

WFP

THE ASSUMPTION underlying our first *Plains Folk* anthology, subtitled *A Commonplace of the Great Plains*, seems, upon reflection, uncommonly presumptuous. We said in the introduction to that book that we wanted to revise the definition of the Great Plains as a region of North America, to consider *what* the plains were rather than *where* they were, to explore regional thought and culture. We proceeded on the premise that there was in the Great Plains an integrity of region, a commonality that might cause people living in any part of this elongate, international, geographical entity to identify with, perhaps even care about, people in the other parts of it. This is a debatable assumption, of course, but that keeps things interesting. We continue to act on the same assumption.

Our essays, in that first book and in this one, derive from our weekly newspaper column, *Plains Folk*. The "folk" part of the title indicates our belief that the best place to look for the culture of our region is in its folklife. Much of the integrity of region we are looking for is the product of environmental influence, and it is in the stuff of everyday life that such influence is most plain. Then, too, this is the sort of material we think we can deal with best, because we are part of it ourselves. We are a couple of Kansas farm (or ranch, Jim keeps insisting) boys with Ph.D.'s. A scholar who loses his roots is a pitiful thing.

So we write, and with our writing we knit together folk experience and scholarly reflection, creating, as we said in our earlier subtitle, a commonplace book of the plains.

Now we come before you with another collection of essays, not a sequel but a continuation of our commonplace. Ever presumptuous, we think that the folk of the plains are interested in looking over even more documents of their region.

Document—now there is a word laden with meaning. Jim's academic discipline is Literature, Tom's History, and both fields are obsessed with documents, or as some call them, "texts." Literature and History belong to the area of

study that academics call the Humanities, a term that nowadays might need some explaining. The Humanities examine the human experience through documents (usually
meaning words on paper), and it is the enviable task of
Humanists to collect and to study these documents. Now,
our type of Humanist should not be confused with the Secular Humanist (i.e., someone who has too much faith in
human nature), the bugbear of the Religious Fundamentalist (i.e., someone who has too little faith in human nature). Oddly enough, however, the scholarly approach we
bring to our subject has something in common with each
of these nonacademic camps. Like the Secular Humanist,
we believe in the resilience, the adaptability of the human
spirit. And, like the Fundamentalist, we believe in our
texts: we revere them as documents of the human experience just as sincerely as a Fundamentalist reveres Scripture
as the Word of God.

A review of our table of contents, however, will show
that the documents we use go beyond mere words on
paper. We have all due reverence for such great literary
texts as John Ise's *Sod and Stubble* or Francis Parkman's *The
Oregon Trail;* and we consult more humble written sources,
such as family memoirs and agricultural bulletins; but
there is more to our region than that. We go after the oral
literature of the plains—the legends, beliefs, songs, and
jokes that folk pass along to one another. We seek the traditions and rituals embodied in everyday activities—working cattle, killing chickens, playing games, preparing food,
chopping wood. And we read, as well, the material culture
of the region—its contraptions, tools, implements, and
structures—the objects that make people effective in their
environment. We say that we "read" these objects because
they, too, are documents. The landscape is our library.

We think it important to accept these documents where
they are and for what they are. For instance, a particular
story or joke told among folk of the plains may be a piece
of fiction, but if it is commonly told, then there is probably
a truth lurking within it: there is a reason for its general

currency, and it is our job to find that reason. Or a particular creation of material culture, say an expensive poured-concrete silo, may contradict what would seem to be wise (i.e., practical and frugal) adaptation for the plains region, but behind its construction, somewhere in the mind of its builder, there is embedded some truth (more abstract, perhaps, than concrete) about the place. These documents can be heavy reading.

That we accept, read, and believe such documents tells you something about us. We are Romantics. We probably belong to the nineteenth century.

A good bit of this Romanticism comes from ancestral and personal experience. If blood tells at all, then Tom, a descendant of nineteenth-century German immigrants, assuredly ought to be a Romantic. Nineteenth-century German Romantics, says Gordon A. Craig, America's foremost historian of Germany, "venerated the origins of things and were fascinated by history"; they also believed the common people to be the genuine embodiment of German culture. This didn't mean they were all happy wanderers, however; they also had a "dark side," Craig says, a tendency toward morbid thoughts of doom. Does this explain why Tom is moved to deep contemplation about his great-grandmother's failed orchard, or about shriveled coyote carcasses hanging on barbed-wire fences?

Jim's Romanticism comes not so much from ethnicity as from occupation—equestrian blood runs through his veins. His grandfather, born in Kansas in 1878, earned his first money herding cattle on open-range Flint Hills prairies. His father and uncle enjoyed local fame for their prowess in both pasture and rodeo arena, his father even participating as a teenager in one of the last Texas-to-Kansas cattle drives. Little wonder that many of Jim's stories concern cowboys, horses, and cattle—or that he enjoys the saddle more than the desk.

Romanticism flourishes for long only where the environment is favorable to it. The Great Plains are such a place. Consider the case of Josiah Gregg, the physician—

turned–Santa Fe–trader who recounted his experiences on the plains in *The Commerce of the Prairies.* "I am almost ashamed to confess that scarcely a day passes without experiencing a pang of regret that I am not now roving at large upon those western plains"; he longed, he said, "to spread my bed with the mustang and the buffalo" and "to maintain undisturbed my confidence in men by fraternizing with the little prairie dogs and wild colts and the still wilder Indians." If you think such ideas passed with the freight wagons of the frontier, then you need to read Craig Miner's history of western Kansas, *West of Wichita,* to see that they survive, thankfully, even in the mind of a late-twentieth-century, bicycle-riding professor from Wichita.

It's no coincidence that, like Gregg and Miner, we get what we think are great ideas for writing while traveling across the Great Plains landscape, by auto or by other means. Some may counter that this is just because of the thinking time imposed by enforced idleness behind the wheel, but that is not so. If enforced idleness were the necessary condition, then our most creative time would be in university faculty committee meetings, and that is an absurd proposition no one would consider. It is the semiarid environment, not the totally arid, that is inspirational.

What we are talking about here is the Romance of the Landscape, the idea that the flat, treeless, semiarid plains have an inexorable effect on how people view the world. Some emphasize the light side, as does Teddy Blue Abbott in *We Pointed Them North:* old-time cowboys tell too many stories of hardship, he protests, "but they never put in any of the fun, and fun was at least half of it." Others dwell on the dark side, as does Andy Adams in *Log of a Cowboy:* "If the monotony of the sea can be charged with dulling men's sensibilities until they become pirates, surely this desolate, arid plain might be equally charged with the wrongdoing of not a few of our craft." This sounds grim, but what could be more Romantic than pirates—or cowboys-turned-outlaw?

For good or ill, the Great Plains provoke, in us and in others, an obsession: the Romance of the Landscape. The documents of the plains tell us so, and we believe them. If we desire higher authority, we may cite Larry McMurtry, whose epic novel of the plains, *Lonesome Dove*, is a Pulitzer Prize winner. His main character, Woodrow Call, is an obsessed man if ever there was one; miragelike, he is "hard to keep in scale"; and naturally he "despised the border, and longed for the open plains."

For sounder authority, by the standards we ourselves have professed, we may cite a steam thresherman from the wheatlands of eastern Colorado. This hardheaded capitalist, with money tied up in machinery and payroll, wrote of himself and his work in 1916: "It is hard to quit. He hears a whistle toot, gets a whiff or two of new straw and grain and can't stop himself, he feels he must go." Compare those remarks with these of a modern itinerant wheat harvester: "Every spring when the first few warm days roll around, you just start counting the days and minutes until you can head south. It is something that really gets in your blood. It'll be a sad day when we quit the business."

We may be extreme cases, but obviously we are not the only plains folk infected with the Romance of the Landscape. We're on the trail of the documents. *Plains Folk II: The Romance of the Landscape* is fresh sign.

Emporia, Kansas   JIM HOY
                                                        TOM ISERN

Part One

PLAINS FOLK AND THEIR LORE

1. *Flint Hills Cowboys*

ELMER COOPER died in September 1986. He was ninety-one years old. Ninety-one years spent in the Flint Hills of Kansas, most of them (except the final few) on the back of a horse, looking after other men's cattle. That's a way of life here in the bluestem, the only life that Elmer and his generation of cowboys knew.

It's a generation that is almost gone. Vic Kirk died a couple of years ago, Turk Harsh last year. Turk was over ninety, Vic about the same. In the Butler–Chase County area where I was reared, the heart of the Flint Hills, E. C. Roberts is the only nonagenarian cowboy I know who is still active. Father of three world champions (Marge, Ken, and Gerald) and former rodeo Man of the Year, Emmett still raises, buys, and sells horses from his home in Strong City.

Elmer Cooper lived south of Saffordville in eastern Chase County. In his younger days he rode broncs at local rodeos, but he, like Harsh and Kirk (both of whom also rode at the local amateur rodeos and celebrations), was a pasture cowboy who never adopted the gypsy life of the rodeo competitor. Not that he didn't have his share of adventures. When he was about twelve years old, he accompanied his father on a horse-buying trip to Miami, Oklahoma. His father pointed his purchases toward Chase County and told Elmer to push them north while he went on about other business. The young puncher took them all the way, nearly two hundred miles, by himself.

Elmer told me once about Vic Kirk's bronc-riding ability, a scene he witnessed at a pasture rodeo back in the days when broncs were snubbed instead of loaded into chutes. Somehow the horse got away from the snubber before Vic was on. With one hand on the horn, the other on the buck rein, and his left foot in the stirrup, Vic pulled himself up past the clawing hooves of the lunging horse and into the saddle, then made the best ride of the day. The late Mason Crocker (who ranched in Kansas, Texas, and Arizona) told me that Vic Kirk was as fearless as anyone he ever saw around horses: "He didn't have a nerve in his body. I've seen him jump into a pen full of unbroken mules with a halter in his hand and come out with a mule and never get kicked."

Turk Harsh was another man who wasn't afraid of anything with hooves and hair. One Fourth of July, in 1920 or 1921, he gathered up fifteen or so broncs and invited the people of Cassoday to bring out their picnic lunches while he entertained them. One after another he rode every bronc in the pen, getting thrown only once when saddle and all came off the horse. I think that Turk remembered every animal he had ever seen in his life. I know that you could show him a picture from 1910 and he would identify the horses first; then he would tell you who was mounted on them.

All three men could tell stories of the old days. Many times I have heard Turk talk about the fun, and hard work, he had had—riding horseback with his wife Marie twenty-five miles (one way!) just to go to a barn dance, playing Halloween pranks, driving cattle for hours through heat, cold, rain, snow. But life never got them down. A friend told me about seeing Elmer gimping around on and complaining about a bum leg a few years ago. "Well, Elmer," my friend said, "you're just getting old." "No, I don't think so," was the reply. "My right leg is just as old as the other one and it doesn't hurt a bit."

It would be tempting to sentimentalize and say that this generation represents the last of the real cowboys. But that wouldn't be true. There are men in their sixties, seventies, and eighties who rode broncs at snub-up pasture rodeos, who rode thirty miles through the dark and the rain to a set of railroad pens to pick up cattle. And there are those of us in our forties who participated in the last of the railroad shipping. Technology changes the externals of cow-

boying, but the center—working with cattle and horses—
remains constant.

It seems that every generation of cowboys (except the
very first, who didn't even know that they were cowboys)
has thought that it missed the Golden Age and that the last
of the real cowboys died out a decade or so earlier. As
Elmer Cooper himself told me once about Shorty Nurn-
berg, another old-time Flint Hills pastureman who died at
ninety-two in 1975, "There aren't any like him anymore."
Nor like Elmer or Vic or Turk or Emmett, but their legacy
lives in the future generations of Flint Hills cowboys.—*JH*

2. *Among the Amish*

THE MOTION PICTURE *Witness* focused public interest on the
Amish, folk who generally shun such attention. Among the
greatest problems of the Amish in the United States is in-
trusion of the outside world upon their simpler, rural culture. The violent plot of *Witness* was merely an overstated
metaphor for that day-to-day struggle of the Amish.

In late January 1986, I spent a day in Yoder, Kansas,
visiting the elementary school, where all the pupils are
Amish. During the morning I told stories to the first- and
second-graders, whose teacher is Peggy Burns, a former
student of mine.

Most of what I saw in the classroom was what I had an-
ticipated. There were the boys in their homemade pants
and shirts, though exhibiting more polyester than I had
expected. There were the girls in their homemade dresses,
coverings, and scarves for recess. I didn't know what to
think of the name-brand sneakers that many of them were
wearing. They didn't know what to think of my Hanoverian German, either. (Although the kids speak English
in school, their first language is Amish low German.)

A half-dozen mothers were visiting. I wondered what

they thought of the stories I was telling. The kids liked the stories about animals—the State Lake Snake, the Anthony Badger, giant flathead catfish, and so on. Better than urban kids, they understood what I was talking about. They also liked the Mexican legends, and those were the ones I was concerned about. Mexican legends are full of Roman Catholicism. But no one seemed concerned.

In the afternoon I sang folksongs to all eight grades of the school. The older kids were more reserved than the younger, who knew the words to "Home on the Range."

It's hard to tell when Amish are disturbed about something. To outsiders they remain inscrutable. The most misunderstood aspect of the Amish way of life is their rejection of modern technologies.

Back East, people think the Amish are queer because they farm with horsepower. Conversely, where Amish settlements have ventured onto the plains, in Kansas and Oklahoma, people think it's strange that they use tractors. The reason the western Amish use tractors is simple and plain: land on the plains is less productive, necessitating larger farm units, requiring more power and machinery. The Amish have to adapt to the land, like everyone else.

Does this mean they have abandoned their religious adherence to simpler ways? Not at all. Outsiders have missed the point of the Amish way of life. The point is not to maintain some permanent, static level of technology, but rather to be different from the rest of the world. The Amish do change, but even in change, they are careful to remain different.

My friend Bill Thompson, a sociologist, explains this more powerfully. The Amish are determined above all to farm and to maintain their rural community, he notes. They recognize that they cannot farm successfully on the plains without machinery. After careful consideration, then, they have adopted modern technologies—not in abandonment of principles but in preservation of them.

Just because the Amish of the plains have accepted certain agricultural technologies, that doesn't mean they have modernized other aspects of their lives. As I left the school in Yoder, children and mothers were climbing into buggies for the drive home.—*TI*

3. *American Owned*

IF YOU TRAVEL much in the southern plains—Texas, Oklahoma, Kansas—you have encountered them. Asian Indians running motels. I've met them in Hutchinson, Kansas; Lubbock, Texas; Liberal, Kansas; in my hometown of Emporia, Kansas. You also have seen the signs at motels, some (like one in Oakley, Kansas) displaying the American flag, all proclaiming they are "American Owned." In Bartlesville, Oklahoma, I even saw one that was "Okie Owned."

A stereotype is developing. It begins with the fact that the motels run by Indians generally are not first-class. They're decent places, but not the best. My observation is that motels bought by Indians have not deteriorated, and some have improved, but an image has developed that identifies Indians with second-class operations.

The stereotype deepens because the Indians are a foreign culture—I mean apparently different from most folk in the region; I definitely do not mean un-American. Most travelers don't know much about the Indians, but they carry away from the motels a collection of casual observations: a scent of curry; an inflection of speech that, although correct, seems hard to understand; the traditional dress of the women; names like Patel and Bakta; a reclusive manner.

Reclusive, yes, and not just in relation to travelers. Local residents also say that the Indians keep to themselves, surrounded by their own family.

So a reaction, a prejudice, sets in. Native-born proprietors of second-class motels (you never see a first-class establishment doing this) appeal to this prejudice by their "American Owned" advertising.

I never stay at a motel that proclaims itself "American Owned," and I know others who think the same way I do. This sort of proclamation repels me for three reasons.

The first is that it is negative advertising appealing to base instincts. If all a businessperson has to say about himself is that he isn't Indian, then he must not have many virtues to advertise.

The second reason is that as a historian I recognize this situation as just one more ethnic-business stereotype on the plains. Jews keep clothing stores, Lebanese are peddlers, Chinese run laundries, Mexicans block beets, blacks are barbers, Greeks run cafés—all these historic regional truisms became truisms because they had origins in truth. But the stereotypes, indiscriminately applied, in time became less true and more bigoted.

The third reason is that as a folklorist I rather enjoy staying at the Indians' motels to see what these folk are up to. What's cooking in there? What's that stuff you're raising in your little garden? Where do you come from? Well, then, how in the world did you get to Hutchinson? Whose are all these kids? These old folks that don't speak English, are they your parents?

I like to know the stories behind the stereotypes.—*TI*

4. Asian Indians and Motels

ON THE EAST side of Emporia, Kansas, just a few blocks from my house, is the Sunrise Motel. Its proprietor is Raju Patel, an Asian Indian.

I would like to make this Indian-run establishment facing east a literary symbol of something, but the problem is that on the west edge of town is the Ranch House Motel, and its proprietor is Kirit Patel, another Indian. That pretty well torpedoes my symbol, and while it floats there dead on the water, here comes a second shot: another In-

dian motelkeeper I have visited with is Hasu Patel, manager of the Sunset Motel in Hutchinson, Kansas.

The story that Hasu Patel told me is representative of
his countrymen throughout the southern Great Plains.
Most of them are named Patel, and most of those who
aren't are named Bakta. It seems to me there are three
main facts to understand about how these innkeeping immigrants fit into life on the plains.

The first is that their journey here is an intercontinental saga reminiscent of that of the Germans from Russia
and other much-persecuted immigrants. Many of the Indians' ancestors emigrated from India to various nations of
Africa, there seeking commercial opportunities. The sojourn in Africa ended unhappily for most. In some places,
as in South Africa yet today, the Indians faced open racial
discrimination. They also saw their business threatened by
governmental instability in the emerging African nations.

So they left, going to Europe or Great Britain perhaps,
but to America if they could get in. They found entry
easier if they had money to buy their own businesses or
had jobs promised them in advance, which explains part
of the motel connection in this region. They left kin scattered around the globe. Hasu Patel has family in India, of
course, and a brother in Zambia.

The second fact is that these Asian Indians are entre-
preneurial folk. My geographer friend Charley Webb says
that the very name Patel connotes a capitalist class. "Most
all Patels are self-employed," says Hasu Patel, and "our
people believe in saving." So the attraction of the motel
business is that it is an accessible small-business opportunity. Hasu Patel, who has a master's degree in mechanical engineering, sought a job in that field first, but then
readily entered his uncle's motel business in Hutchinson.

Third, the Indian immigrants are intensely loyal to
their families. They take care of their own, refusing government handouts, and raise their children strictly. Hasu
Patel has brought his aged parents to live with him. He also

has the two children of his brother from Zambia, because the brother thinks they can get a better education here. One more reason the Indians like the motel business is that it can be run as a family enterprise.

All this makes quite a composite: homeless immigrants seeking opportunity, establishing homes and businesses, gathering and cherishing their families, spurning charity or government patronage. If these folks were light-skinned Protestants, every Republican politician in the country would want to have his picture taken with them.

So I ask you: Which motels are truly "American Owned"?—*TI*

5. *Just Joking*

BECAUSE OF the diversity of peoples who compose the United States, Americans have a persistent and often tacky tradition of making fun of one another. Ethnic and cultural differences have provided inspiration for countless riddles and anecdotes of the kind that I call "jokes of denigration."

What is behind this sort of humor? Folklorists generally attribute it to anxiety. People make fun of other, different cultural groups because in some way they feel threatened by them. Jokes of denigration relieve the anxiety.

The American experience provides many examples of this. The great Irish immigration of the 1840s and thereafter provoked a vast repertoire of Irishman stories, many of the Pat-and-Mike variety. Poles among the so-called new immigrants of the early twentieth century were likewise the focus of Polack jokes. At heart, older-stock Americans were a little fearful of Irish and Poles who practiced Roman Catholicism and competed for industrial jobs.

Ethnic humor also flourished regionally on the plains. The legendary Ole and Lena, for instance, were the central figures of classic anecdotes about Norwegians told by their non-Norwegian neighbors in the Dakotas. A funny thing happened to these Norwegian jokes, however. After Norwegians became successful, comfortable, and acculturated, they appropriated the jokes as their own—telling them on themselves. It seems that the jokes have become a standard of success. By telling them, Norwegians say to one another, "Look how far we have come."

The same goes for the old stories told about stingy Welshmen in the Emporia, Kansas, vincinity. Welsh people now tell these on themselves. (Example: a Welshman finds a fly in his soup and picks it out; instead of throwing it away, he shakes it vigorously, crying, "Spit it out! Spit it out!")

Recent jokes of denigration have focused also on other ethnic groups. Tim Kloberdanz (he of the cardboard stalking horse in the "Duck Tales" portion of this book) says that American Indian jokes have become common in North Dakota. ("What do you call five hundred Sioux at the bottom of Devil's Lake?" begins one. "A good start" is the answer.) He thinks the vicious jokes are perhaps a reaction to Indian claim cases against the U.S. government.

On the central and southern plains the new cultural groups on the scene are immigrants from Mexico and Indochina. Like other immigrants in American history, these peoples have clustered where there are opportunities for industrial labor; Garden City, Kansas, home of an Iowa Beef Producers plant, the largest slaughter facility in the world, is a notable example. Mexican and Vietnamese jokes are rampant in the locality.

Plains dwellers also poke fun at cultural distinctions other than ethnic. Texans in general, and graduates of the University of Texas in particular, are likely to refer to College Station, home of Texas A & M University, as "Malfunction Junction" and to denigrate the Aggies mercilessly.

At the other end of the plains, Montanans for some reason find the whole state of North Dakota hilarious, particularly its flat, treeless character and its sparse, agricultural population. "What's the official state tree of North Dakota?" they ask. "The telephone pole," they reply. Or they tell about the sign on the North Dakota border that reads, "Drive Carefully—No hospitals for 250 miles in any direction."

If jokes of denigration are a measure of anxiety, then here is a logical question: just what about Aggies and North Dakotans makes you UT grads and Montanans so nervous?—*TI*

6. *Sick Jokes and Vile Songs*

QUITE A FEW of my acquaintances and students know that I am a collector of all sorts of odd folklore, including jokes, and they report things to me that they have heard. Still, I was not quite prepared for one type of humor they brought me: Ethiopian jokes.

Most all Americans have seen television portrayals of the sad situation in famine-struck Ethiopia, and judging by some of the humor I have heard, it has aroused some guilt feelings that people try to relieve with jokes. The Ethiopian jokes, and I have heard more than thirty different ones, take the form of riddles. "What's the world's fastest land animal?" goes one. "The Ethiopian chicken," is the answer.

Most people consider this humor sick, and perhaps I do, too, but then adolescent humor—and these jokes do seem to be moving mostly in junior high schools—is pretty tacky.

What surprised me even more, however, was when people began reporting farmer jokes. These focus on the farm-debt crisis, and they can be quite bitter. "How can you tell the difference between a dead coyote in the road and a dead banker in the road?" one riddle asks. "There are usually skid marks in front of the coyote."

"What's the difference between a farmer and a pigeon in the machine shed?" another one inquires. "The pigeon can still put something down on a tractor."

These jokes illustrate something about folklore in our contemporary world: that in order to survive in a society of mass media, folklore has to be so scurrilous that it cannot travel through respectable print or electronic media and is forced into the channels of word of mouth. An outstanding example of this comes from the plains of North Dakota. Friends there sent me a tape of a song called "Freedom Fighter Gordon Kahl."

Gordon Kahl was a member of the Posse Comitatus, a paramilitary organization that likes guns and hates income taxes. In February 1983, Kahl and his followers killed two United States marshals near Medina, North Dakota. Kahl escaped in an unmarked police car.

There ensued a manhunt that lasted until June 1983, when federal marshals and FBI agents located Kahl at a house in the little town of Smithville, Arkansas. Kahl died in the house after a smoke bomb set off an arsenal inside.

North Dakotans, like people across the country, were initially horrified at the bloodletting in Medina. The news was traumatic enough that it produced some sheepish humor. People thought it was funny, for instance, to telephone a crowded restaurant and have the manager page Gordon Kahl.

North Dakotans were particularly intrigued to hear gossip that someone had written a song memorializing Gordon Kahl as a "freedom fighter." Curious talk about this song became so intense that the manager of a radio station in Fargo, receiving an anonymous tape of the ballad through the mail, decided to play it on the air. He presented the ballad with a stern editorial to the effect that it was "a vile song, a song of fractured logic and misguided emotional fervor."

The station manager was appalled that North Dakotans might accept Gordon Kahl as a hero because he was an underdog and he tied his cause to a deep-seated belief of many Americans: that government had grown too large, powerful, and expensive. Kahl said that the income tax was an instrument of tyranny and the devil. The nameless balladeer who wrote "Freedom Fighter Gordon Kahl" picked up on this theme. Said he of Kahl, "When he saw his rights were shattered, / He knew deep inside it mattered, / And the choice was shoot or let them steal it all." Said the radio station manager: "We all identified with Gordon Kahl, if ever so discreetly."

My conclusion is this: that "sick jokes" and "vile songs" are more normal than sick. They don't mean that plains folk are ungenerous to Ethiopians, unsympathetic to farmers, or disdainful of law and order. They are just symptoms of uneasy feelings about matters beyond our control.—*TI*

7. *Just Scandalous*

OH NO, my wife says, he's starting with the jokes again. But it's not my fault. My boss, a fellow named Dallas Roark, is a Baptist whose daughter goes to Baylor University. Every time he visits Waco he comes back to Kansas infected with Texas Aggie jokes, like old-time longhorns carrying Texas fever. So Dallas says to me, "Do you know what were the Lord's last words to the Aggies?" I don't know. "Play dumb until I get back."

A few days later I walk into a hotel in New York city and there's Dave Danbom, from Fargo, North Dakota. A Swede. He says to me, "Do you know what were the Lord's last words to the Norwegians?" You'd think jokes like that would be stopped at a port of entry somewhere.

I have written before about such monuments to popular taste as Aggie jokes, Norwegian jokes, Ethiopian jokes, and farm-crisis jokes. Other types, such as the AIDS jokes, are too gamy for me to touch even for the sake of analysis. (Well, maybe just one. Did you hear about all the dead alligators washing up in Florida? Gator-AIDS.)

It always amazes me how swiftly this scurrilous stuff, which has to go by word of mouth because it isn't fit for respectable mass media, spreads, often leaping almost instanteously from the coasts right into the heart of the plains. Like the shuttle jokes—lots of sick ones commemorating the explosion of space shuttle *Challenger*—"Make that a Bud Light," and so on. All of which goes to show that the modern plains are in no way isolated from the rest of the world, its events, its fears, its insecurities.

My hometown of Emporia lately has gone through a trauma it considers its own unique affair. I say "affair" advisedly because I'm talking about disclosure of a love triangle—no, it's a quadrangle; no, it's more than that, so just call it a polygon—involving, among others, a Lutheran minister (Tom Bird), his congregational secretary (Lorna Anderson), her husband (Marty Anderson), and a couple of brothers named Carter.

The minister's wife and the secretary's husband (who was heavily insured) both died under suspicious circumstances, setting off a long series of investigations. The minister and the secretary were both sent up to Lansing, but lots of questions remain as to who killed whom for whom.

The matter shook up the community, not only because the main characters were people you would expect to be respectable, but also because the messy trials threatened to soil the reputations of various political and financial pillars in town. There was continual talk that the county attorney had a list of Lorna's lovers and was going to call them all as witnesses.

No laughing matter? Wrong. The jokes permeated the town like the smell of our IBP packinghouse. I call them "ABC Jokes," naming them for this comment by a burly patron of a local cowboy bar: "Do you know your Emporia ABCs? Anderson, Bird, Carter. . . ."

I had this collection of ABC jokes when Calvin Trillin, a big-time writer for the *New Yorker*, came to Emporia to write up the case, and we talked about the jokes. He mentioned me and them in his piece in the magazine.

Afterward my mail brought a packet of stuff from Frank Moorhouse at Wolfson College in Oxford, Australia.

He wants to trade collections. It seems that a Seventh-day
Adventist pastor and his wife came back from an outback
camping trip with the report that a dingo dog had carried
off their baby, but really they had killed the child themselves, and now dingo baby jokes are rife.
Scandalous, yes, but not unique.—*TI*

8. *Rural and Urban Legends*

A RESPECTED older farmer was out with a bunch of hands
pitching hay onto racks. Suddenly, he clamped a death
grip on his pants leg and yelled, "Snake, snake, come quick
or it'll bite me!" The hands gathered around and helped
him slip off his pants without releasing his grip. Then he
turned loose and dropped, along with his pants, his spec-
tacles case.

This classic legend I found in an 1881 *Butler County*
(Kansas) *Democrat*. How do I know it's a legend? Because
the reporter insisted, "This incident occurred in Spring
township, and is a true story." When the teller insists an
outlandish story is true, it's a legend; otherwise it's just
a tale.

The same newspaper in 1882 mentioned one of my
favorite legends, the old saw about "Thirty Quails in Thirty
Days": "With the opening of the quail shooting season the
man who can eat thirty quails in thirty days comes to the
front," remarked the editor. "We hear of him every year,
but somehow we never hear of him accomplishing the feat.
He eats them in his mind." The editor offered to bet $1,000
against the likelihood of some "man with a cast iron stomach" eating a quail a day for thirty days.

I should feel a little insulted, since my Grandpa Dune-
kack was one plainsman who swore he had done just that.
(Come to think of it, those quail finally did do him in.
About forty-five years later, at the age of ninety-five.) In-

stead I wonder whether this stricture is supposed to apply to southern-plains scaled quail, too, or just bobwhites.

Now that the days of pitching loose hay and hunting for subsistence are past, rural legends like these have expired. A new generation arises, however, applied to modern (mostly urban) circumstances. Take for example this story of suburbia. (My friend Julie Johnson says "it really happened" to Dorothy Brinkman's sister-in-law's friend.)

A woman was preparing tuna salad for a luncheon. Her cat got into the tuna and ate part of it, whereupon she threw him out of the house. The luncheon guests arrived and ate, and meanwhile, a man ran over the cat in the street. He carried the dead cat to the door, but looked in a window and saw the luncheon going on, so he just left the cat out on the lawn.

After the guests had left, the woman came outside and found her dead cat. She immediately called the guests and told them they had eaten bad tuna. They all went to the hospital and had their stomachs pumped.

("The Legend of the Bad Tuna": making up the titles for these things is half the fun.)

Now—think about this one the next time you go to your car in a dark shopping mall parking lot. This woman finished her shopping late at night and went out into the nearly empty parking lot. As she was about to get into her car, she noticed an old lady sitting in the backseat. The poor lady said she was tired, and she had climbed in there to rest, and could the woman with the car drive her home?

The woman said she would, but first she had to run back into the store, where she had left her credit card. Once inside, suspicious, she called the police. The police dragged the old lady out of the car, but she was no lady— she was a man in a dress, and on the seat beside him was a hatchet.

I like the Hatchet Lady legend, because I can imagine it doing all sorts of good for our downtown business people.—*TI*

9. *Bigfoot*

DRIVING HOME from Bismarck, North Dakota, a few years ago, we figured McLaughlin, South Dakota, would be a good place to stop for breakfast. Oklahoma Mike Everman was along. He has to eat every forty-five minutes or so. He had this lunch bucket, and he would clank the handle of it to make a sound just like the falling lid of a self-feeder makes when a pig pulls its head out. So we stopped at a café called, like about ten thousand others, the Cozy Kitchen.

Which is how we learned about the genus Bigfoot, species South Dakota. At the Cozy Kitchen the two breakfast specials were the Pheasant Hunter and Bigfoot Pancakes. Jim had the Bigfoots: size 18 flapjacks with clearly delineated toes. A sleepy waiter without the flair for publicity to match his menu explained that this vicinity of the state had acquired some fame for sightings of a great hairy creature people called the Bigfoot.

So the summer of 1986, en route to Saskatchewan, I decided to find out what ever happened to this Bigfoot. I suppose I approached this with a bit of cynicism. If you look in the library for a book about Bigfoot phenomena, you find it shelved in the 001s with works on UFOlogy. If you look under "Bigfoot" in the *Reader's Guide to Periodical Literature,* it refers you to "Animals, Mythical." And I'll admit that up to this time I had read most of what I knew about the Bigfoot while waiting to check out groceries.

Still I had to look into it. The Bigfoot of the North American northwest, commonly called by the American Indian name Sasquatch, frequented the forests of California, Oregon, Washington, British Columbia, and Alberta. The Bigfoot of the Himalayas, generally called the Yeti, was a creature of high, mountainous terrain. What was this "Animal, Mythical," doing in the middle of the plains?

I turned west off Highway 12 onto gravel so as to explore some of the creature's reputed turf on the way to

Little Eagle, a few miles south of McLaughlin. People had told me that a trader named Gary Alexander in Little Eagle could inform me about the Bigfoot. Little Eagle is on the Standing Rock Indian Reservation and near where Sitting Bull was killed.

It's a stereotypical reservation town—run-down government housing, muddy roads, laundry on lines—and something out of the ordinary, too—brush arbors erected in many yards. I soon saw that a powwow was going on and the brush arbors were for entertaining visiting kin.

The dancing was going strong, and so was a slow-pitch softball game pitting two reservation teams. I asked an Indian policeman where to find Alexander and he gave me directions, but when I got to the place, I found about an acre of pickups ahead of me and figured it was not a good time for an interview.

I eased back onto the highway toward McLaughlin, stepped on the gas maybe a little too hard and long, looked up to see the lights of a reservation police car flashing in my mirror, pulled over, and waited. Here came the same Indian cop who had given me directions. "You really want to know about the Bigfoot?" Sure, I said, a little relieved.

"Well, I got a fellow on the radio you ought to talk to. He was the one who led the hunt for the Bigfoot back in '77. I'll tell him where to meet you, if you say so."

And that's what we did.—*TI*

10. *After the Bigfoot*

VERDELL VEO is a big fellow, well over six foot, stocky, one imposing Sioux cop. Bureau of Indian Affairs people on the Standing Rock Reservation have described him as a model reservation policeman. With him is a short, chunky sidekick, another Indian policeman named Bobby Gates.

To the north rises Elkhorn Butte, a well-known landmark. As its base runs a wooded creek, and closer still to us is the softball field, whence outfielders chase fly balls in our direction. I sit on the tailgate of my pickup, Veo and Gates lean against vehicles, and we talk about the Bigfoot. The Dakota Bigfoot is seven foot or taller, heavily built, brown or black in color. He can run as fast as a horse, and behind him he leaves, of course, toed footprints sixteen or eighteen inches long, spaced six to eight feet. He bellows and shrieks at night. He eats skunks and other varmints. He stinks.

From August through December 1977, a hundred or more people in the vicinity of Little Eagle reported sighting the Bigfoot—towering above the bushes along a road, peering into windows, running through pastures. Veo took plaster casts of the footprints and collected feces samples. Various people photographed it, or him (the pronoun remains variable).

Gates himself encountered the Bigfoot at his home near Fort Yates, North Dakota. "I was working outside and I had a feeling that someone was watching me, over by the corral. His hips were way above the corral. I called another officer, Selven Yelloweyes, and we tracked it over to our neighbor's, and there was a herd of black Angus heifer cattle. He went right in there and crouched down like he was trying to hide. Then he just turned around and stood up, and with gigantic strides he walked right over the hill."

"I got pictures of dogs that were killed," says Veo. "A four-wire fence, it took the two top and the two bottom wires and stuck that police dog in that barbed wire and wrapped him up in it. That was a damn good police dog."

The officers believe the creature, although wary of men, especially men with rifles, is strangely attracted to women and children. One night they built a bonfire, the women of the community gathered around it, and the armed men searched the vicinity. "My lady friend had a portable radio and I had one," recalls Veo. While the men hunted fruitlessly, "she called me and said he was standing by the bushes, watching us, right now."

The most chilling encounter, however, was up on the

Elkhorn. Veo spotted a Bigfoot on the butte, and so after dark, while Gates watched from below with a night scope, Veo led a search party up. But there were two creatures there, not just one.

"You can see the top of the trees over there," Gates points for me. "That one was right over there, he was luring one of the officers up there. The other one came circling around and trying to cut him off. I was here with the night scope. So I hollered, I said, 'Hey, there is one trying to cut you off.' So they started to come back, and that one tried to cut him off, but they got back to the vehicles in time."

Veo explains, "I had a feeling, or instinct you might say, that no weapon I would have been carrying [he had a tranquilizer gun] would have made any difference. . . . I'd better get out and just leave things alone."—*TI*

11. *The Bigfoot Legend*

THE DAKOTA BIGFOOT is a legendary creature. When *Newsweek* reported the story in 1977, the magazine used the headline "Legends: Bigfoot is Back" and implied that the whole affair derived from superstition or fraud. That's not what I mean by "legend." I mean that this is a fantastic story, told for fact, that may or may not be so.

Bigfoot hunter Gary Alexander of Little Eagle said "it's almost a matter of honor" that the Bigfoot legend be substantiated. "We've taken too much criticism to forget it." Having no honor at stake, I don't care. The truth of a legend is not the events behind it, but the telling of it. Legends may be fiction or nonfiction, but they are all true.

There are several things to learn from the telling of the legend of the Dakota Bigfoot. One has to do with racism. Except for Editor Merle Lefgren of the *McLaughlin Messenger,* people off the reservation were quick to ridicule those on it who claimed to have sighted the Bigfoot. After all, not only were the reports fantastic, but they also were coming from people with names like Chasing Hawk and Uses Arrow. According to *Newsweek,* the reports "began to gather respectability" only after "a couple of prominent local ranchers" (not Indians) spotted the creature.

A second lesson is that renowned legends such as this one bring out the worst in people bent on glory or profit. Whether for honor, as Alexander said, or for fame, as was the case with professional Bigfoot hunters who descended on the Standing Rock Reservation, most folks on the scene assumed that it was all right to shoot the Bigfoot in order to obtain a corpse as evidence of his existence.

I asked Verdell Veo about this, and he said his goal was either to tranquilize the creature with a dart or to "wing him" with a rifle. Here is a critter people say is cunning and malicious, and the hunters, at night even, are supposed to "wing him"? Compared with the rifle toters (and even a group of bowmen from Nebraska), the dealers in Bigfoot pancakes and Bigfoot T-shirts and Bigfoot bumper stickers, although tacky, were harmless.

The third lesson from the Bigfoot affair is that people tell legends. Whether those who told saw a Bigfoot, saw something they mistook for one, or just made the whole thing up, they told.

They told because people need to tell things. Career policemen of the Bureau of Indian Affairs had nothing to gain from the telling, but Verdell Veo and Bobby Gates told me their stories.

Various writers about the Sasquatch, or Pacific Northwest Bigfoot, have explained the phenomenon as a vision quest of American Indians. The Dakota affair convinces me that these observers are right—not that the vision-quest idea is particularly applicable here just because the people involved were Indians, but that it is generally applicable to all of us. We all need to tell fantastic tales from personal experience.

The only difference among us in where we get the tales. Some of us recount revelatory visions received atop lonely peaks; some of us testify about Quiviran kingdoms in cleaning products or health foods; some of us wax epic

about high school championships and sweethearts won
or lost; and some of us go up the Elkhorn after the Bigfoot.—*TI*

12. *Stalking Geese*

It's HARD for young folks to impress old-timers with feats
either of work or of play. Marksmanship is a case in point.
I remember that my Grandpa Isern, although too gentle to
be an enthusiastic hunter, nevertheless watched with interest when in the course of a morning's feeding one of the
boys would take a shot with a .22 at a fleeing rabbit. He was
just waiting to say, "Huh—I could have had that one with a
good throwing rock."

If by chance the rifle shot connected, Grandpa was still
ready with the head-shaking comment, "Must have been
a sick one," hearkening back to the old folk belief that to
shoot and bag a slow-moving or sitting rabbit was to risk
exposure to rabbit fever.

The only venatic accomplishment that impressed either
Grandpa Isern or Grandpa Dunekack was killing geese.
Goose hunting on the flatlands presents a problem for
hunters (such as me) without big spreads of decoys: there
are too many open, level fields where geese can light, feed,
and look with disdain on human predators trying to stalk
them. Any geese I shot came at the expense of a long crawl
and by the grace of an intervening tumbleweed.

What made me think about all this was reading an article from February 10, 1910, reprinted in my old hometown paper, the *Ellinwood* (Kansas) *Leader*. This item reported that a local man, Walter Herold, had shot four
Canada geese. He had noticed a flock landing in his corn-
field, whereupon, the paper reported, he "took a horse
and worked his way to within about 40 yards from where
the geese were sitting, and when they got up he shot four
out of the flock."

I doubt that this account of Herold's stalk makes sense

to many modern readers, but it does to me. Grandpa Dunekack once explained to me how men in the early 1900s used horses to stalk geese. The hunter would start a horse walking, grazing some, along a line that would pass within gun range of a feeding flock. The hunter walked alongside the horse, bent over, using the horse as a screen. Finally, he stood and either stepped behind the horse to shoot or fired over the horse's back.

The geese, although sharp sighted, evidently were unconcerned about the approach of a six-legged horse. They were by this time accustomed to feeding in cornfields, into which stock frequently were turned after picking season. Whether the horse remained equally unconcerned about someone firing a shotgun over his back, I don't know.

As best I can determine from various state and federal officials, stalking geese with horses never has been prohibited by law. One of the people I asked about this was Jim Ross, from the Minneapolis office of the U.S. Fish and Wildlife Service. He mentioned the topic at a staff meeting in Minneapolis, and several people there seemed familiar with the practice, one of them even describing how northern-plains hunters trained their stalking horses.

Because I grew up in the age of tractors, I never had the opportunity to test this folk method of goose hunting; we never had a horse on the place. Still, I'd like to try it. Since Jim seems to be something of an authority on horse trailers (see our earlier *Plains Folk* book), maybe I can get him to haul a suitable goose horse out into the flat country for me next fall.—*TI*

13.   *Duck Tales*

IT WAS a mistake to mention my interest in stalking horses to Tim Kloberdanz of Fargo. He proceeded to tell me how, as boys, he and his brother had stalked a flock of geese by hiding in a big cardboard box cut into the shape of a horse.

He said they painted spots on it to make it look like an Appaloosa. I believed the whole story until he came to the part where he and his brother popped out of the box and started shooting their cardboard shotguns.

Well, Tim, did I ever tell you about the last time the neighbor kid, Rollie Wayne, and I went duck hunting? It happened like this. We had located a fine spot out in a milo stubble field, flooded by recent rains, where big flocks of late-season mallards were pitching in. It was a perfect setup for an open-field Great Plains duck hunt.

Early in the morning we got out there, dug a little hole to put our feet in, and built a tumbleweed blind around the place where we would sit. We left our shotguns there while we, in our hip boots, scattered a couple of bags of decoys in the shallow water.

It was just getting light enough for shooting and we had finished setting out decoys when we looked up to see a great flock of mallards approaching like a thunderhead. We splashed back to the blind and began loading our guns quickly.

I was using a three-shot pump gun, but Rollie, sort of an antiquarian, had his granddad's muzzle-loading sixteen-gauge. He really had to work to get powder, wad, shot, and cap in place before the ducks dropped in.

Then we popped up to shoot. Looking for the green heads, I dropped a drake with each shot—three ducks down. I heard Rollie fire, but I didn't know to what effect until we had waded into the water to retrieve the birds.

I tossed my ducks onto the ground and looked back to see my hunting partner dragging something through the water that looked like a bale of hay. When he got the thing onto dry ground, I came over to examine it, but at first I couldn't figure it out. It looked up close like a cluster of ducks stuck together somehow.

Rollie started picking ducks off the bunch and continued until he had a pile of fourteen birds at his feet. In his hand he held a straight, thin stick.

Suddenly I understood. Rollie had become so excited

when that big flock came in that he had jumped up and fired as soon as his gun was loaded, neglecting to withdraw the ramrod. The ramrod flew out among the ducks, and they were so thick it skewered fourteen of them. There stood Rollie with his fourteen ducks and I with my three. He was grinning. What could I say about a shot like that?

I took another look at that pile of ducks, assumed a scornful manner, and said, "Shoot, Rollie, what kind of shot was that? Why, two of those birds are hens."

And we haven't gone duck hunting since.

Now you tell one.—*TI*

14. *Prohibition Stories*

PAT O'BRIEN, one of the historians here at Emporia State University, is currently working on a study of bootlegging in Kansas. (Pat always said that Kansans would vote dry as long as they could stagger to the polls, but the 1986 vote on liquor-by-the-drink proved an exception.) Recently I went along with him to do some interviewing. We were going to talk to someone who had also done quite a bit of cowboying in his day, and I wanted to ask some questions about that, but I also picked up some good bootlegging stories.

One story was about a farmer and a rancher (I'm keeping everyone anonymous throughout this chapter) near Matfield Green in Chase County, Kansas, both of whom were pretty good distillers of "canyon run." They were sitting around, drinking and lamenting, for this was 1917 and Kansas had just voted to go bone dry. Before that time it was illegal to make or sell booze, but possession was permitted. Kegs and cases would often pile up at depots around the state, I was told, while the stationmaster would sometimes sample the wares (or peddle it to his friends) if the owner was slow taking delivery.

But to get back to Chase County. As the two men got

mellower, the rancher told the farmer that he had voted
for prohibition. Why? asked the farmer. Because, was the
answer, some people can drink and handle it, like me. But
some people can drink and can't handle it, like you. The
farmer cussed him a little and they both sat there and kept
on drinking.

My father and others have told me about one woman in
Cassoday who ran a hotel and sold what was popularly
known as "sheep dip." Another local bootlegger would
drop bottles of varying sizes next to fence posts as he drove
into town at night for a dance. If a cowboy at the dance
wanted a pint, the two would drive out on one of the back
roads and the bootlegger would stop at a fence post, kick
around a bit, and come back with a bottle. No matter how
dark the night, he had an uncanny sense for remembering
fence posts.

This same dealer kept his big jugs buried under fence
posts in his corral at home. The law often came looking,
but they never thought to take the wire off a post, lift it out
of the ground, and look in the bottom of the hole. I recently read of a bootlegger in the Texas Panhandle who,
after spending a few weeks in jail when he was convicted of
selling whiskey, decided that it was safer to sell maps instead of booze. So he sold two-dollar maps, five-dollar
maps; whatever size you wanted, but he was nowhere near
when you dug up the liquid gold where X marked the spot.

Another Cassoday cowboy who made a bit of pocket
money selling what he didn't drink made the mistake of
not burying his bottles deep enough. A lawman walking
through his corral stepped on a neck and the rest of the
bottle tipped up, so the cowboy went to work on the county
road crew for a few weeks. The road gang was building
fence along the ranch of one of his drinking buddies. The
rancher, out feeding his cows, saw his friend and came
over to talk. The two of them arranged for the cowboy-
turned-road-worker to leave a couple of post holes unfilled
each day. The rancher, when he was out feeding his cows
each morning, would then drop a pint into the last hole

and kick a little dirt over it. When the road gang got there, the cowboy would clean out that hole first, slip the bottle into his pocket, and stay happy all day and all night. It was probably the most enjoyable sixty days anyone ever spent in jail.—*JH*

15. *More Prohibition Stories*

A LOT OF bootleg made in Kansas came from the Little Balkans, the pit-mining country in the far southeast corner of the state. This "deep shaft," as it was called, was famous nationally and beyond for its quality, and its makers took pride in their products. If you got a bad batch, you just poured it out and told your source about it when you went back. It was replaced, no questions asked for good customers.

Getting the goods from manufacturer to consumer took some ingenuity, for lawmen soon learned to spot a car that had been rigged for hauling deep shaft. One man, who lived in Greenwood County, had a false bottom in a horse trailer. His horse was never ridden, but it averaged several trips a month to southeast Kansas or Missouri. Another whiskey runner worked with a helper. The helper drove a big fancy car while the bootlegger had an old clunker. They would load the clunker with booze, the big car with cow feed from a feed store and have it take the lead on the return trip. Lawmen would see the big car traveling low to the ground and would pull it over. The driver would act suspicious, stalling when requested to open the trunk, and the lawmen would give him their full attention, waving the old clunker, with its load of liquid corn, on by.

One of my favorite stories is about a bar in deep-shaft country with a sign over the door that proclaimed in big letters, "Kentucky Bill's Place," and in smaller letters under it, "I run it." One time a drunk was giving Bill a hard time—arguing, trying to start a fight, being generally obnoxious. Bill quietly took it until his brother showed up. When he walked in the door, Bill handed him a bucket and asked if he would go out and pump some water. When the brother came back in with the water, he asked Bill, "Here it is, now what should I do with it?" "Pour it on him," Bill replied as he picked up an ax handle from behind the bar and calmly cold-cocked the loudmouth.

Another story, which I have heard from several sources who have set it in a variety of places, a sure sign that a story has gone into the folk tradition (even if it actually happened), concerns a garage in southeast Kansas that was serving as a front for some bootleggers. People would drive their cars in to be "fixed" and drive them out loaded with booze. One time a federal agent drove his car in, knowing full well that there wasn't a tool in the place and that the people there couldn't have changed a tire, much less fixed an engine.

They knew he was a fed, of course, just as he knew they weren't really mechanics, but his brazenness went a step beyond accepted behavior in the protocol of bootlegging. So when he complained of a knock in the engine and asked smugly if they could fix it, one of the bootleggers opened the hood, looked at the engine and said, "Hey, Tony, this engine has some loose pistons. Bring that sledgehammer over here and I'll tighten them up!"—*JH*

16. *Singing Joe Gray*

ONE OF THE arguments for consolidated schools a generation ago was that larger schools could offer the full range of special subjects, such as art and music. So how come nobody can sing anymore? William Allen White, the great Progressive editor, sang in a street quartet as a boy and

later wrote of his generation, "All the world seemed singing." My generation can't sing and can't play any instrument except the radio.

Joe Gray was of W. A. White's generation. From 1930 to
about 1953 he ran the Arkansas Market at 615 Main in
Eureka, Kansas. At this store, and outdoors during summer, he sold all manner of fruits and vegetables he trucked
into town himself from neighboring states. He had two
trucks, one named *Prosperity* and the other *Depression*.

Understand that Eureka was a cosmopolitan place.
It led the state in oil production for a while during the
1930s, and the streets were full of roughnecks and Baptists
from Texas and Oklahoma. Newsboys worked Main. From
one of them the question "What's the news, Perk?" would
prompt the chant "White woman marries a rig-builder!"
Big laughs and good tips followed.

Joe Gray joked with the customers, too, but besides
that, he sang. I asked his daughter, Velma Wheeler, what
his singing was like, and she said, "It came from the heart."
She also gave me copies of his songs. Some of them he
wrote, some he just adapted. True to the tradition of the
English broadside, he had his songs printed up on cards
and put them into bags of groceries.

Fearless, this fellow Gray. He sang "Way out West in
Kansas" complete with the verse about Cross-eyed Pat
("When she cries, she's a total wreck, / The tears run down
the back of her neck."). To the tune of "Marching through
Georgia" he rendered a satire on aging Union veterans of
the Civil War, with the chorus:

> Hurrah, hurrah, you ought to see my dad,
> He was the bestest soldier that Uncle Sammie had.
> For he whipped the rebbles and you bet he whipped 'em bad,
> While they were marching through Georgia.

Other songs poked fun at Italians, Germans, Irishmen,
and Mary Pickford, but Gray saved his best ammunition
for politicians. His theme song, "Prosperity," to the tune of
the prison song "Ninety-Nine Years," was inspired by a ra-

dio address of President Herbert Hoover. Hoover, who insisted that the depression would end if people would only accentuate the positive, had appealed for someone to write a prosperity song. Gray's was probably not exactly what the president had in mind:

> It's stocks and it's bonds and it's large corporations
> That's caused great distress to God's own creation.
> It's pooling of wealth and it's pooling of wheat,
> That's why we're all hungry with plenty to eat.

As for Hoover, Gray thought it was time for a change:

> If you want prosperity, why you'd better hurry,
> Get right with your God and elect Bill Murray.

Alfalfa Bill Murray was the tobacco-spitting governor of Oklahoma who wanted the Democratic nomination for president in 1932. I don't know why Gray liked him, but I would put up with any kind of politics if I could have a grocer who sang.—*TI*

17. *Barn Dances*

ONE OF THE most common forms of community entertainment in the Great Plains of times past was the barn dance. I seem dimly to remember being at these old-fashioned dances, but probably I just remember hearing about them. We did hold a few dances in barns when I was a youth, but most of our dancing was done in someone's garage and we used phonograph records (rock-and-rolling to Carl Perkins and Little Richard) instead of a band. Real barn dances, with live fiddle music and someone calling squares, ended with the generation before mine.

I learned quite a bit about barn dancing a short time back while visiting with one of my neighbors south of Emporia. Harry Potter was born in Chase County, Kansas, in 1900, moving one county east to his present home in

1940. When he was in his late teens, he and his brothers formed a band—Bill on violin, Jack on guitar, and Harry on either of those two instruments. None of the brothers could read music and none did any singing. Instead they picked up their music by ear, learning much of it from their father and his family, the rest from going to dances where other bands were playing.

Much of the dancing back then was square dancing. Sometimes Jack Potter would quit playing to call a square, although more often a caller would be in attendance and would do the honors. There was no electronic amplification of either instruments or voices. Other popular dances were the waltz, the schottische, and the two-step.

Not all community dances back then were held in barns, I learned. In fact, Potter distinguished among several varieties of dances: barn, platform, house, quarter, and invitation. Barn dances were most often held in spring and fall and were usually open to the entire community, although men had to pay a quarter to get in (thus the term "quarter dance"; women had free admission). House dances were held in the winter, the furniture in one room being moved out to make way for the band and dancers. Often house dances were also "invitation" dances because of the limited space. Even here, however, men had to shell out their quarters to get in; the band, after all, had to be paid. Platform dances were almost invariably open to the public and were held on specially constructed wooden platforms in the open air of summer.

Dances usually began around eight or nine in the evening and would break about midnight for a "lunch," sometimes sold by the entrepreneur who was sponsoring the dance. At that time the dancers would often pass the hat to entice the band to keep playing. Potter told me that he usually got about three or four dollars for a night's playing that literally paralleled the roosting of the chickens: "When I was playing for house dances, I would get home when the chickens were getting off their roosts. My father would say, 'Where have you been all this time?' and I'd say, 'Well, I'm just getting home; they finally quit dancing.'"

Not everyone in a community danced, and those who didn't sometimes made moral judgments on those who did. Potter said that when he and his wife, Cleo, first moved to Emporia, they went to a function at the rural school their daughter attended. There they met a man who said to them: "I guess I been the heathen around here." How so? asked Potter. "Well, I play for dances." "So do I," Harry told him, "but I don't claim to be a heathen."

Potter played his last dance sometime during World War II, but he still has fond memories of those times. He certainly gave me an excellent perspective on barn dances from the point of view of the musician.—*JH*

Part Two

ANIMALS, WILD AND DOMESTIC

SEVERAL YEARS AGO my father-in-law (Wilbur Thompson) gave our daughter and son a burro. Like most gift animals of the equine species, this one also had a catch: we had to drive from Emporia, Kansas, to Valley Mills, Texas, to get him. Wilbur had read in a farm magazine about the Wild Horse and Burro Adoption Program and had signed up for a couple of "free" burros (one for his son's children, also).

This adoption program (which has since received much notoriety, courtesy of network television broadcasts of wild burros being airlifted out of the Grand Canyon) is an attempt by the Bureau of Land Management to lessen the numbers of rapidly multiplying mustangs and burros (and thus lessen the problem of overgrazing on public lands) without turning them into dog food. I don't know how many hundreds of dollars it took to catch (humanely, in contrast to the grim methods used by Clark Gable and Mongomery Clift in the Arthur Miller film *The Misfits*) and transport the various animals from Wyoming and Idaho and Arizona to the holding station in Texas, but the purchase price is a bargain—around a hundred dollars (primarily to cover vaccinations and other health expenses).

We arrived at Valley Mills early enough in the morning to see several dozen mustangs and burros being sorted, inspected, and branded (a freeze brand that denotes age and a "born free" status that prohibits use of the animal for commercial purposes). The two invoice sheets we had been sent each listed ten animals, ranging in age from four months to thirteen years. Each animal was labeled for sex and color—F (female) for jennies and S (stud) for jacks. Colors listed included brown, black, gray, and pink. Our animals, a gray jack and a pink jenny (she was a buckskin with a definite pinkish tinge), both two years old, loaded easily and rode home without incident. The rush-hour traffic on the Dallas–Fort Worth Interstate seemed to be much more unnerving to me than it was to them.

We kept the jack (thinking he might need more taming than the jenny) and the kids named him Elroy. I fully expected him to be wild, but after a short adjustment period he proved to be as tame as a dog and an excellent pet. He didn't lead too easily, but he soon took to being ridden and would let us catch him anywhere. He had come from Arizona, but we decided that he was not an alumnus of the Grand Canyon airlift: airplanes didn't scare him, but a horseback rider did, especially one swinging a rope.

The jenny (the cousins named her Beth) never did tame down. Not only was she hard to catch, but she would also kick and bite. One time she picked up my brother-in-law's dog and shook it the way a rat terrier shakes a rat. Which explains why sheepmen like to have burros around—apparently they do the same thing to coyotes. Beth got traded for a shetland pony, but we still have Elroy. My uncle and my father have kept him most of the summer, hoping for some mule colts next year, but we'll bring him home before long. I miss the sound of his nightly braying.—*JH*

19. *Mules*

IN THE LAST CHAPTER I wrote about our not-so-wild wild burro, Elroy, and mentioned that both my father and my uncle were breeding some mares to him. Not that either one of them needs any more animals around their respective places (in fact, one of Dad's mares has already had two mule colts from Elroy), but I think that mules are a reminder (pleasant or otherwise) of their younger days. Mules were also part of my own unbringing—I might be the only English professor in the plains who has cultivated corn with a team of mules.

My grandfather, like many farmers in the earlier twentieth century, had a large herd of horses—some for work, some for riding, some for trading, and some for breeding. Dadhoy kept a Percheron stud for many years, I am told, although I don't ever recall seeing any workhorses around the place. Instead we had Flossie and Tessie and Andy and Mickey. The first two were a team of mare (or molly) mules that Dadhoy worked on the go-devil and, later, when we got a farmhand stacker for the tractor, my sister or I drove to rake hay.

I'm not sure why the other two mules were a team, unless they were the only two available at the time they were broken. Mickey, a white mare, was as energetic as the brown horse mule was lazy. A switch or a stick, constantly applied, was the only way to make him pull his share of any load. But if Andy was lazy, at least he was tractable. Mickey, on the other hand, was touchy. She hated to have her ears touched, and even after a full day's work she could jerk you right off your feet if you didn't pull the bridle off just right.

After the Percheron stud, my grandfather kept a jack, a Mammoth (which threw bigger mule colts than did the little Spanish jacks). One of the first trips I remember going on as a child was to Fort Scott, Kansas, to look for a jack, and my first memory of Dadhoy's barn was the picture of a donkey's head that Uncle Marshall had drawn on the door of the oats bin.

Our jack was named Old Black Joe, after the Stephen Foster song, and we kept him for several years after Dadhoy died and we were no longer raising mules. Then one summer he got out into the horse pasture and bred three of our mares, including Dad's best cowhorse. Some of my friends helped us break those mules to ride, but I think Dad sold them to a horse trader before we ever broke them to harness. The last mules we worked at home were a pair of buckskins, a horse and a mare we had raised from my old kid horse, that could walk about six miles an hour. Dad used them as a feed team until the mid-1960s before selling them to a rancher from the Nebraska Sandhills.

I mentioned earlier that we have two young mules, progeny of Elroy and a little mouse-colored mare. They are both buckskin mares, a three-year-old (Wynona) and a yearling (Naomi). My son has the older one broken to ride and is working on the younger one (who did a pretty good job of bucking the first time he tried her). We thought that if they were gentled down some it might be easier to find someone to break them to harness in a couple of years. Not that we will have any work for them to do, but after all, mules are a reminder (pleasant or otherwise) of my younger days.—JH

20. Bull Tales

DINNER-PARTY conversation in cattle country might not be as genteel as it is in the suburbs, but it's probably more interesting. A short time back my wife and I were visiting with a group that included several people who made most of their living working with cattle, and as the evening grew late the stories grew better, especially a string of bull tales. Now, while bulls are indispensable to the cow business, they can also be an aggravation, which was the gist of the episodes recounted.

The stories started when a man who had raised nothing but Herefords all his life told about his first Texas longhorn bull, which he had bought to put on some first-calf heifers. Getting the bull home proved to be an adventure. It seems that the stock racks of a pickup just aren't tall enough for the leaping abilities of a longhorn. As the new owner was driving along he felt a lurch, heard hoof beats over his head, and realized that the bull was about to jump over the front of the stock racks onto the cab of the pickup. Some quick brake work, artful swerving, and fast engine gunning managed to get the bull back into the bed of the pickup, but every few minutes the bull would give another leap and the man would have to jerk the pickup around again, all this with a big eighteen-wheeler on his tail. He knew that he was not going to get the bull home unless he got him tied down, so with one hand he fished a lariat off the gun rack and got a loop built, then gave the pickup a last, big swerve before braking to a screeching stop, jumping out with rope in hand, and just barely getting the rope on the horns and the bull pulled down and tied off before he made his escape.

This story got another man, a breeder of longhorns, started. He told first of a visitor who had gone fishing in a pasture full of longhorns that were used to being fed protein pellets. One old pet cow mistook the bait bucket for a feed bucket and came on the dead run from a quarter of a mile away, headed straight for the hapless angler, who tossed poles and worms into the air as he dived back into his car.

This rancher also told of having a couple of novices out to help round up his herd one day. The bull didn't want to leave the pasture and after some chousing around got a bit sullen and refused to move. The helpers then decided that maybe throwing some rocks at him would do the trick, so one of them got off his horse and began picking up rocks. The bull, apparently not relishing the prospect of being the target of Chase County flint rocks, thought this a good time to move, so he did—straight toward the source of potential harassment. The would-be rock chunker was first alerted to danger only when he felt the sudden jerk of bridle reins slipping through his hand as his horse left in a cloud of dust. Both horse and man outran the bull, whose heart was probably not really in the chase.

My own favorite chase story occurred about a dozen years ago and concerns a friend who wanted to move a bull. This friend was neither a cowboy nor a farmer, but he did own some land where he raised a few sheep (his wife was a weaver) and where he had started a small but nice herd of Charolais. He wanted the bull moved from his cow pasture to the barn lot about half a mile away, so he asked me and one of my English-department colleagues, whose grandfather had given him a good paint horse, to help. The bull owner had an old saddle, probably picked up at a farm sale for twenty dollars or so, and was mounted on a small sorrel horse that knew nothing about working cattle. On the first turn through the rocky, brush-filled pasture, the cinch broke on his saddle, which went flying through the air, rider still firmly in the seat. Nothing if not intrepid, he jumped back on bareback, and on the second turn—or maybe the third—the bull, which must have weighed close to a ton, got contrary and ran into a dense thicket of sumac and locust.

The owner jumped off his horse and disappeared into the thicket yelling, "I'll bring him out!" He did, all right. In a matter of seconds the owner came charging out, bull hot on his heels (like Will Geer leading the grizzly bear to Robert Redford in the movie *Jeremiah Johnson*), yelling, "Here he is!"—*JH*

21. *Blabs*

A FEW WEEKS AGO we weaned a couple of colts that were born last spring, and I was reminded of just how noisy that job can sometimes be. With our calves we have no problem because Dad usually sells them right off the cows and they can do their bawling for their new owners. The mares, however, have to be kept around for a few days if they are giving much milk so that they can be nursed and have the pressure on their udders relieved as they dry up, which, needless to say, increases the whinnying on both sides of the barn door. After a few days, however, we will move the mares to another pasture and the colts will soon become self-sufficient. Still, weaning can be a problem, especially if the stock owner is softhearted. I remember a few years back breaking a four-year-old mare for a neighbor. When I went to get her, I discovered that not only had she never been broken to lead but also that she was still nursing her mother. Fat and sassy.

But often the lack of weaning is not the result of hu-

man negligence or sympathy. Sometimes a yearling, running in a pasture of cows, will revert to its calfhood and start robbing the baby calves. More rarely, an old cow will rob the calves, or even nurse herself. A device known as a blab is often used in situations like the above. About the time we were weaning our colts, I was rummaging around the barn on the home place and found half a dozen blabs, three of them commercially manufactured, three homemade. They were of two general designs. The first type was a tin flap made to fit into and hang down over a calf's nostrils so that it could graze and drink but couldn't nurse. One of the boughten blabs (about six by four inches) even had a series of four V-shaped notches that would poke into the cow's udder, causing her to kick the offending animal away. The other manufactured blab was smaller (three by five inches) and lacked the sharp points; it was made by the Keeb company of Beatrice, Nebraska. Two of the homemade blabs were also of the flap type. One was small (about three and a half by seven inches), the other, perhaps built for a cow, was larger (five by eight inches). In addition to their slicker appearance, the manufactured flaps differed from the homemade ones in their mode of fastening. Two spring-held arms fit into the nostrils of the animal wearing a boughten blab; a heavy wire piercing the septum kept the homemade ones in place.

The other two blabs were designed to fit around the nose and be held in place by a halter or a chain around the animal's neck. Around the bottom rim of this type of blab was a series of teeth pointed out and down in such a way as to allow the animal to eat and drink but to cause it to be kicked away by any cow it tried to nurse. The manufactured halter blab was calf size (it measured a little over four inches across), had seven teeth, and had a slot for a chain. It was called the SO-BOSS and was made by Simonsen Iron Works at Sioux Rapids, Iowa. The homemade halter blab (five teeth) seems to have been intended for a cow, measuring seven inches across. A leather halter (now fairly stiff) had been specially built and riveted onto it.

Whatever the design, and whether homemade or
manufactured, the blab was intended primarily for barnyard, not range-country, use. Weaning three or four calves
is one thing; weaning three or four hundred is something
else.—*JH*

22. *Yokes*

A FEW DAYS AGO my son and I helped my father haul some
calves to market, along with a couple of cows he was cull-
ing. One old cow was wearing a homemade metal yoke, a
visible reminder of the breachiness of her younger days.
"Breachy," for those who might not know the term, is what
farmers and ranches call an animal that crawls through
fences, one that will not stay in its own pasture. A yoke
is a folk device used to help keep these dissatisfied cattle
at home.

Yokes have been in use for centuries. In this country,
for instance, Pehr Kalm, a Swede who visited Pennylvania
in the mid–eighteenth century, observed pigs wearing tri-
angular wooden yokes and horses dragging large forked
sticks from their halters in order to keep them from step-
ping over low fences.

The simplest kind of yoke, like those worn by the Penn-
sylvania pigs, is a wishbone- or Y-shaped branch cut out
of a tree. I remember several of these from my youth.
They were usually about two inches in diameter and made
of hedge or some other tough wood. The V part of the
wishbone was wired onto the cow's neck just behind her
head, two prongs of the wishbone pointed down between
the cow's legs, nearly touching the ground. Thus, whenever she poked her head under, between, or over a barbed-wire fence, the yoke would hit and keep her from
crawling under, pushing between, or jumping over the
wires. Usually.

The metal yoke on the cow we were shipping was one

Dad had constructed from some flat metal straps salvaged from an old windmill. It was made of two nearly identical parts that bolted together around the cow's neck. One piece fit on the top of the neck, the other on the bottom. Each piece looked a little like a large U with a straight extension protruding from the middle. These extending pieces were about a foot and a half long with about three inches of each tip bent forward (away from the cow's body) at a right angle.

I recall another metal yoke we had around the place for years, one that was made of small round bars (less than half an inch in diameter). It looked very similar to the one Dad had made, except that it had two sharp prongs about three inches long just where the extending arms joined the U-shaped pieces on both the top and bottom of the neck. These sharp projections were pointed back toward the cow's body so that when she put her head through a fence and brought pressure to bear on the yoke, the prongs would bite into her neck and cause her to pull back.

This particular yoke was not homemade but one sold commercially. As such, it was not constructed quite as solidly as our homemade one. Dad makes things to last—two or three nails where one will do. Instead of bolts, the store-bought yoke was held together by a cotter pin. Today that yoke is lost somewhere in one of our pastures, or perhaps just across the fence in a neighbor's pasture—wherever the cotter pin broke.

We took the yoke off the cow we sold the other day. Whether or not she was still breachy I don't know. She got her reputation, and her yoke, years ago and wore both for as long as she remained on the Flying H.—*JH*

23.   *The Town Pasture*

I SOMETIMES THINK about the nearly lost art of milking cows and how, fifty or seventy-five years ago, nearly every farmer on the plains had half a dozen or so cows so his family could have milk to drink, feed for a few pigs or bucket calves, and cream to sell for a little cash flow. City dwellers got their milk delivered daily in glass bottles back in those days, while people who lived in small towns usually had fresh milk.

One way they got fresh milk was through a local milkman, someone who, like Pat Bullock in my hometown, lived near the edge of town (but then everyone in Cassoday lives near the edge of town) and kept a few cows in a nearby pasture. I can still remember seeing him, morning or evening, walking out to get the cows. Unlike ours, which were usually as far away as they could get, Pat's cows always seemed to be at the corner of the pasture, waiting to be let out for the short walk along the edge of the highway to the milking shed. Pat had several steady customers to whom he would then deliver fresh milk.

Other small-town residents, however, would have milk cows of their own, which they would keep in the "town pasture." Many towns had such a pasture, one owned privately but available, at a reasonable charge, to local people. Emporia (where I now live) had one, I am told, just beyond West Street, which is now just about the geographic center of the city.

The town pasture at Washington, Kansas, was (or had been) owned by the bank there and was called both the bank pasture and the common pasture. This latter term carries associations of the English custom of the commons. British farmland in earlier times was privately held, but the grazing land of a particular village was common to all.

The late Harold Durst told me about a man named Earl Moore who lived at Morrowville, Kansas, up near the Nebraska line. As a boy Moore was hired to look after the milk cows in the common pasture. During the colder months each family kept its cow in a barn and fed it hay and grain, but during the pasture season, which ran from May 1 to October 1, Moore had to bring the cows in each morning, then take them back out after milking. Each eve-

ning he repeated the process, receiving for his labor a dollar a month per cow. Not bad wages for a teenager during
the Depression.

So far as I have yet been able to discover, however, my
home town came closest to the English custom of the commons. Much of the town lies in the northwest corner of a
section of grass known to everyone even today as the Cassoday Pasture. In my memory this pasture has always been
leased and stocked in the ordinary fashion, but in earlier
years townspeople could keep a milk cow there without
charge. Just when this custom began, or how long it lasted,
I don't know. My father says that Billy Mercer held the
lease on the grass around the turn of the century and that
he was a good-hearted man who didn't mind letting the
Texas steers he was pasturing share the grass with a few
local Jerseys and Guernseys. There was a small set of pens
at the northeast corner of town, and apparently owners
would take turns bringing the cows in for milking. Who
knows, if refrigeration and faster automobiles hadn't come
along, people in the plains might still be drinking cow-
fresh milk.—JH

24. More on Town Pastures

IN THE LAST CHAPTER I wrote about the common practice
in many small plains towns of maintaining a town pasture.
Here city dwellers could, usually for a small fee, keep a
milk cow, often employing a local youngster to bring all the
cows in each night and return them to the pasture the next
morning. Thus many townspeople enjoyed fresh milk at a
reasonable cost. I have since learned in my travels around
Kansas and the plains of several more town pastures.

As pointed out earlier, William Mercer, who for years
leased the pasture that surrounds my hometown, didn't
charge the half-dozen or so cow-owning local residents
for letting their bossies share the grass with Texas steers.

Beyond his innate charity, Mercer's generosity may have stemmed from the ancient English custom of the commons, a system whereby farmland was held privately but moors and other rough grazing lands were open range for anyone in the village. His father, after all, had come to the Flint Hills from the county of Kent in southern England.

I have not learned of any other town pastures where cattle could be kept without cost, but the situation at La Cygne, Kansas, fits into the tradition of the English commons in another way: the town pasture there was turned into the city park, according to Wayne Hardisty, who, when he was twenty-six years old, moved to La Cygne from Salina to open a variety store. Two years later Hardisty was elected to the city council and was, in his words, "responsible for opening the gate on that pasture."

The forty-acre pasture, located in the south part of town and policed by the city marshal, was, to put it mildly, not overgrazed. Only a single cow and her calf (owned by Jack Crogan) were still being kept there (by that time, 1942, not many people still did their own milking), and community use of the property was already shifting focus. Picnic tables had been built in the pasture, along with a stone cabin for the Boy Scouts.

This shift reached completion the evening two little girls wanted to have a picnic in the pasture but found the gate locked (the mayor had a key, as did the owner of the cow). When Hardisty heard of their plight, he suggested that the pasture be turned into a park. Today, in addition to the Scout cabin and the picnic tables, there are hookups for campers, a hangar and airstrip for the local flying club, and, of course, playground equipment for children. It seems to me appropriate that acreage once used by the community for nourishment of the body has been transformed into a place of repose and relaxation—acreage for nurturing the spirit.

There was a rather unusual town pasture situation at Junction City, Kansas, which abuts the military reservation at Fort Riley. Local officials there agreed to educate chil-

dren of army personnel in Junction City schools in ex-
change for letting townspeople keep milk cows on fort
property. This arrangement was mutually advantageous
for many years, but then people quit milking. So, as the
numbers of students grew while those of cows declined,
the city could no longer absorb the expense and the old
barter system was scrapped. Today houses fill the area between Pine, Ash, Madison, and Eisenhower streets where
milk cows once grazed.—*JH*

25. *Wintering Horses*

I DON'T THINK a winter has gone by in the ten years since
we moved out to the country that someone hasn't asked me
how we take care of our horses in the cold weather. When
I say, "We don't do anything; they take care of themselves,"
I often get incredulous stares and sometimes even implicit
threats of reports to the SPCA: "What? You didn't put
them in the barn and feed them during that big snowstorm
and below-zero weather last week?" What people don't realize is that horses, at least those that have been allowed to
have some sort of normal life outside a box stall and the
show ring, are tough animals.

We always had a good-sized herd of horses and mules
around home when I was growing up. In the winter we
would keep one team of mules (for hauling feed to the
cows) and a saddle horse or two around the barn, feeding
them oats and hay. The others we would turn out into a
nearby section pasture, letting them fend for themselves
(just like mustangs). My sister and I would always want to
take them some hay, but Dad would say that they were
better off without it, that if we started feeding them they
would just stand around and wait for more instead of digging through the snow to the old grass. Besides, he said,
as long as they were eating snow-covered grass, they were
getting plenty of moisture. If we fed hay, we'd also have

to break ice in the pond. Invariably, when we got them in along about the first of April, they would be in good condition. They might not have been in shape for heavy work, but they would be lively enough to crow-hop around the first time they were ridden. Deep snow and cold weather hadn't hurt them a bit.

I must admit that I am a little more solicitous of my horses now—I feed hay beginning in January and usually start giving them protein pellets a month of so before spring grass comes—but they do run outside no matter what the weather. A few years ago we had a long spell of below-zero weather, so I put a couple of the younger horses in a box stall and left the barn open so that the remaining three or four could get inside. Next morning the free-running horses were covered with sleet and snow; they had preferred the outdoors despite the weather. In fact, the ice on their coats was a clue to the reason that horses don't require much pampering in winter. Horses are well insulated and not much of their body heat will escape to melt the snow and icicles clinging to their hair. It looks cold to the human eye, but the horse is warm.

Now I'm not saying that horses can be turned out anywhere in October and forgotten until April. There has to be plenty of forage in the pasture and they have to have access to moisture of some sort. If there is no running water or no snow, for instance, and the weather is so cold that a pawing hoof can't break the pond ice, then someone will have to break it for them. Some kind of windbreak is also desirable. Generally speaking, however, horses are much easier to winter than are cows. It was the cattle that died by the thousands in the Blizzard of 1886, not the mustangs.

A few years ago I ran a little experiment. We had four horses around that winter. Two of them I left in the pasture on their own, the other two ran to a spring and were fed grain and hay all winter long. Around mid-March we brought the two pasture horses in. They were just as well fleshed and lively as the pampered ones. And they had certainly used a lot less of my time, energy, and money.—*JH*

26. *Guinea Hens*

I'M VAGUELY ANNOYED when I pass a place where people keep peafowl. These birds are worthless, dirty, and obnoxious, and I can't understand why people harbor them. I always suspect that people who have peafowl in their yards also have poodle dogs in their parlors.

On the other hand I'm biased in favor of folk who have guinea hens, those more modest members of the order *Gallinaceae*. We kept a few guineas when I was a kid, mostly the common gray pearl variety, and a few of the exotic white ones. Grandpa Isern said they drove the rats away, but I don't understand just how.

I probably shouldn't say we "kept" guineas. Generally they wandered off and foraged, and if they happened to roost in the yard, it was because that was the only place with trees for them to roost in. Guineas are independent birds. They refuse shelter, fly like pheasants, hide their nests, abandon their clutches should humans disturb them, and attack the faces of persons bold or thoughtless enough to approach their broods.

Guineas have other virtues besides their yeomanly independence. Poultry specialists whose works (dating from 1862 forward) I have read point out that guineas are watchful. When they see a hawk, they sound an alarm to save more sedentary barnyard birds. They clean bugs off squash and cucumber vines. They are faithful, preferring to mate for life. The keets (baby guineas) look like quail chicks—real cute, but of course, you can't pet them.

Unfortunately, most of the virtues of guineas are not economic. Few Americans have a taste for dark guinea flesh. If you ask me, it's awful—all the gaminess of wildfowl but none of the character. Besides, if you want to butcher one, it's impossible to catch; you have to shoot it. Most people object to the cries of the birds. The male's call is a simple shriek. The female says, depending on whom you ask, either "buckwheat, buckwheat" or "come back, come back." I am dubious the call sounds like either phrase, but I am certain it does not sound like a gentle good morning.

If anyone cares, there's a fascinating history behind the guinea hen. The fowl's ancestral home was west-coast and northern Africa, whence the ancient Greeks and Romans brought it to Europe. The bird subsequently disappeared in Europe until historically recent times, after colonization of the Americas. European colonists had carried the guinea hen, along with human slaves and okra and other cultural truck, from Africa to the sugar islands of the West Indies. Next reintroduced to Europe, the guinea assumed commercial important in France and Germany, then traveled to mainland North America, probably via both Europe and the Caribbean Islands.

In the United States the guinea found broad favor only in the South, including the southern plains states of Texas and Oklahoma. Guineas are few north of Kansas, both because different sorts of people settled there and because the climate is too cold for African birds that roost outside.

There was no compelling reason for northerners to be concerned with guinea culture, because no great market for the birds existed in America. Early in this century a guinea vogue developed in the Northeast; fashionable hotels there traditionally had served grouse and other wildfowl, and when game laws ended market hunting, the hotels began foisting roast guinea on the rich and famous. One hotel in New York reportedly used three thousand guineas during the first four months of 1905. This market never swelled to significance, however.

So guineas are relegated to the status of farmyard oddities. But if you're keeping oddities, better guineas than peacocks.—TI

27. *Dogs and Pickups*

SOMEHOW IN THE agricultural history of this country farming and dogs got wrapped together like the strands in a
piece of barbed wire. I know from reading old manuscript
census returns that this was so at the earliest settlement of
the plains; every farm had a couple of dogs. These days
any farmyard you drive into, a bunch of dogs are barking.

I guess there are such things as useful dogs—dogs that
heel cattle, herd sheep, point birds, or run coyotes. But I
suspect that most farm dogs, a century ago or today, are
about as worthless as the succession of canines I grew up
with. People tell you they're watchdogs, but since they bark
for any reason or no reason, I can't see they're much good
for sounding the alarm.

The only reason for keeping these animals is amusement. Lots of farm work is lonely and repetitive, and a dog
is better than no entertainment at all. It's not that dogs are
natural comedians. They're funny because they have to live
with people and with all the befuddling contraptions farm
people use.

Like pickups. Dogs always went to the field, but in
horsepower days they could keep up running along. Now
they have to ride. And they like it. We had one dog so
obsessed with riding that when people started a car, he
jumped onto the trunk.

Jumping into pickups is a way to mark stages in a dog's
life. It must be a thrill for a pup the first time he makes his
run, jumps, gets his front legs in, and then, reaching, gets a
hind leg over the top and falls in on his face, all without
human help.

The decline of a dog's life comes when he no longer can
get that hind leg over the edge. The key to aging gracefully is to persuade people to open the tailgate without
begging. The proper approach to this is to stand behind
the pickup and feign indifference. Eventually someone will
open the endgate, of course, but even then it's best to re-

main reluctant. Make people plead with you to hop in, and they'll be more considerate the next time. Acting indifferent isn't easy, because when it comes to riding, dogs of all ages are adolescents. There's so much to see, and usually the best stuff is on the other side, making it necessary to run back and forth and peer out, ears snapping in the wind.

The chill factor is severe in an open pickup bed during winter. My father recognized this by allowing certain favored dogs into the cab. They soon took this for granted and even developed eccentricities about it. One insisted on sitting by the window, another liked country music on the radio. Every time Charlie Pride came on he'd whimper and lick all over the inside of the windshield. I still don't understand that.

One dog didn't ride in the cab, because he preferred to ride on top. I mean on top of the cab. This started because we would load bales in the back and stack them as high as the cab. Dogs always ride on the very top of such stacks, and this one developed the unnerving habit of walking across the cab and looking upside down into the front windshield. Then he took to jumping up on the cab even when there were no bales on back.

He took a couple spills off the cab at forty miles per hour or so, but only one resulted in serious injury—a leg broken near the hip. We took him in to the vet, Killer Tyson. Killer fixed him up with an aluminum splint everyone said couldn't possibly work, but it did. If you opened the endgate the dog could jump in the pickup with the splint. When he got it off after six weeks or so, sure enough, he hopped back on top of the cab.—*TI*

28. *Turtles and Horny Toads*

In 1986 the Kansas legislature named an official state reptile—the ornate box turtle—to go along with our state bird (western meadowlark), state animal (bison), state tree (cottonwood), state flower (sunflower), state insect (honeybee), and state song ("Home on the Range"). I haven't done a survey, but I doubt whether many other states have outdone Kansas in naming official emblems. There is even a movement to name the channel catfish the official state fish. (I'd prefer the bullhead myself; it might not have much glamour, but it's a survivor and it beats any other fish for taste.)

Actually if we must have a state reptile the box turtle is not a bad choice; considering that the matter was handled by politicians, it might have been the mossback snapper or even the prairie rattler. Mythically speaking, turtles have a good reputation (helping to bear up the earth, winning races against hares), and they are useful eaters of insects. On the negative side, they can wreak havoc among the tomatoes and strawberries in a garden and they contribute, albeit unwillingly, to messy highways.

Turtles do make great pets. Is there a kid anywhere that at one time or another didn't keep a turtle in a box, if only until his mother found it under the bed? Dick Robbins of Pratt told me that when he was growing up he had a huge turtle collection—over three hundred in a pen in his backyard; he made his dad stop for every turtle he saw along the road. Other people have told me about turtles marked by paint or by carving on the shell that would return year after year to the same yard.

My own favorite reptile is a lizard that is commonly called a toad—the horned (or, more colloquially, "horny") toad. Despite the forbidding appearance and the proclivity when upset of squirting a thin jet of blood from the eyes, horned toads are gentle creatures and very colorful. I had one for a pet when I was younger, one we had found in a pasture a couple of miles south of home.

Although most prevalent in the Southwest, horned toads are found from Canada through Mexico. They are relatively rare in my part of Kansas, although I have found one just a few miles south of Emporia and I have seen several in the Flint Hills east of Cassoday. I remember as a boy reading an article in *The Cattleman* about a Texas writer with a pet horned toad (named Old Horny) that stayed around his desk and caught flies.

You would expect the horned toad to be common in Texas, but apparently loss of habitat and extensive use of pesticides (which curtails their food supply) have greatly reduced numbers there. Not to mention the sale as tourist-trap curios of live horned toads or dead ones embedded in plastic. The situation is serious enough that Texas nearly twenty years ago declared the horned toad an endangered species. Ace Reid, the wit and hand behind the well-known "Cowpokes" cartoons, has also gotten serious and has founded the Texas Horned Toad Association in an effort to save what happens to be his favorite reptile, too. I hope his campaign affects people as successfully as does his sense of humor.—*JH*

29. *Sparrows*

AT ONE POINT in John Ise's wonderful memoir of home-steading on the central plains, *Sod and Stubble,* Henry Ise, the father of the German family, lapses into a sulky silence. Finally he remarks, "I heard something today that I haven't heard for many years—not since I left the Old Country."

"What was that?" the children wonder.

"Sparrows," Henry says. "We always had so many there, in every stone building; and I thought I would never hear one again." A tear appeared in his eye.

To Henry Ise it was a good omen that English sparrows, or house sparrows, introduced to North America some forty years earlier, had found their way to his homestead on the plains. His remark, however, is the only kind comment I have ever known anyone to make about these birds.

My Grandpa Isern, gentle soul that he was, nevertheless was always happy to supply me with .410 shells if I would use them to kill sparrows. It annoyed him to have the birds around the sheds and coops. My father, trying to raise irrigated milo, was even more vexed by them. He always said he didn't mind them eating their bits of grain, but he couldn't stand the way they would sit atop a head and "pick, pick, pick," eating some, but knocking more to the ground; it was the waste he protested.

Despite Henry Ise's sentiments, the English sparrow won universal notoriety as a pest in the United States and Canada. A bulletin of the United States Department of Agriculture said in 1916, "The English sparrow among birds, like the rat among mammals, is cunning, destructive, and filthy." According to this indictment, the bird consumes grain, ravages gardens and orchards, displaces songbirds, defiles buildings, and to top it off, "has no song, but is noisy and vituperative."

Agricultural scientists urged farmers and townsmen alike to thin the sparrow population through a variety of ingenious means. A simple way was to pour out a string of grain for bait, then use a shotgun on the birds that lined up to dine. Various kinds of traps captured birds alive, some by luring them into what looked like good nesting orifices, others by baiting them into screen traps. Periodic destruction of nests and eggs was direct and effective. So were FFA pest contests (see our first *Plains Folk* book).

In Boston in 1889 an organization called the American Society of Bird Restorers, concerned that sparrows were crowding out their songbirds, employed six men a month to destroy sparrow nests. Isn't it just like Bostonians to hire people to do their dirty work for them?

There is a simpler solution, but Americans seem repulsed by it. In Asia and in southeastern Europe, house sparrows are sold in open markets and prized as food. I haven't tried one, at least not knowingly; there is a legend in the family that my elder brother Dave once slipped a sparrow breast in with a batch of turtle doves by calling it a "young one."—*TI*

30. *Blackbirds*

HAVE YOU NOTICED the blackbirds? As you drive across the grain-growing regions of the southern plains in fall or winter, look up at the flocks strung out above you. Look either way along the string of birds—you can't see the end of the flock. If you're driving parallel to its line of travel, you'll drive ten, twenty miles, and still perhaps not leave the flock behind. Look across the stubble fields, and the feeding birds, leaping from ground to air and dropping down again, appear serpentine, as if the flock itself were a great creature, the birds mere cells.

These birds, intriguing as they are, have become a major animal pest of the plains in two ways. First, their destruction of crops, particularly sunflowers. Spokesmen for the National Sunflower Association say that although sunflower raisers in 1983 spent three million dollars to fight the birds, they still caused ten million dollars' damage. Other farmers also suffer losses from the birds, but not as much as sunflower raisers do.

Second, their concentration in winter roosts, often in urban areas. I don't know about allegations that roosting blackbirds cause animal and human disease in the localities of concentration—this sort of talk is emotional and often biased—but the aesthetic effects of urban blackbird concentrations are obvious. Municipalities seem powerless to disperse them.

The United States, according to the Fish and Wildlife Service, has a rather stable population of about a half-billion migratory blackbirds (redwings, yellowheads, grackles, and cowbirds). The problem is not that the population has increased, but that it has shifted to new areas, especially the plains. This is a problem created by human initiative. It comes from the expansion of irrigated feed-grain culture from the 1960s to present. Some plains people blame the increase in blackbirds on reservoirs and wildlife refuges, where they often see the birds congregating, but this is out of order. It is the feed that holds the birds in the region.

Farmers use various devices—shotguns, automatic cannons, shiny objects, mechanical scarecrows—to frighten the birds from their fields, but this does not solve the overall problem. Birds frightened off one field just fly into a neighboring one. What the National Sunflower Association wants is for the Fish and Wildlife Service to obtain special funding from Congress for crash programs to reduce the number of blackbirds, employing either chemical sterilants or what it calls "lethal agents"—poisons, in other words.

Poisoning is a bad idea. If live blackbirds are a health hazard, then dead blackbirds are a worse one. Sterilization, on the other hand, might be a solution, if it can be directed selectively. Sterilants administered in roosting areas might deal with the blackbirds without significant effects on other species.

There is a flaw in this line of reasoning, however. If the problem is not population but the new location of the birds, then reductions in population can produce relief only in degree, and I doubt that Americans desire extermination of such creatures as red-winged blackbirds. Great populations of blackbirds on the plains resulted from changing land use; it may be that they will disperse only when land use changes again.—*TI*

31. *Carp*

"HE'S A BIG ONE, whatever he is. I think he's a catfish. He feels like a catfish. There he is—nope, he's a carp." What a disappointment.

Little Cheyenne Creek, just a couple miles north of where I grew up, was a muddy, smelly stream. Folks say it was not always so, but I don't remember it otherwise. It is, like most other streams in the grain-growing parts of the plains, chronically turbid. It also has its own peculiar problems in that parts of it have been rechanneled into sterile ditches and in that it serves as the outlet for the Cheyenne Bottoms. That saline marsh feeds it tons of carp.

Why the disappointment at hooking a big old carp? Isn't this *Cyprinus carpio,* the German *Karpfen,* object of intensive aquaculture in Europe since at least the 1200s? Isn't this the creature we see in Continental cookbooks, its head still on, surrounded by dainty garnishes, staring at us under the heading "Karpfen blau"?

The carp, originally an Asian fish, indeed has a long history as a food for European peoples. It was an ideal fish for fish farming, because it thrived under pond culture. Americans familiar with its high regard and economic importance in Europe brought the fish across the Atlantic in barrels. The first documented case of this was in 1831, when a fellow named Henry Robinson brought a few dozen carp to New York, releasing them first into his own ponds, then into the Hudson River. The legislature even protected the fish, imposing a fifty-dollar fine for destroying them.

During the 1870s the United States Fish Commission, a federal agency, made carp introduction a high priority. Its aquaculturalists pointed out that nearly all the native fishes of North America were carnivores, and they believed that the most expeditious way to increase fish production was to introduce a substantial vegetarian fish, the carp. They shipped carp all over the country, intending them mainly for pond stocking, but of course the fish escaped to lakes and streams, too.

During the 1880s carp were a fad. In 1883 the Fish Commission sent stockers to 9,872 applicants, representing 298 of the nation's 301 congressional districts. Nobody wanted to be left out, least of all the people of the plains. They realized that their rapidly developing region was short on game fish and on fish habitat. Newspapers of the region trumpeted the carp as tasty and as eminently adaptable—even to the less-than-ideal waters of the plains, the implication was.

The promoters of carp were half-right. The fish were adaptable and soon ubiquitous. The streams teemed with them, but the carp quickly wore out their welcome. "With persons who had been able to obtain in abundance many species of our finer native fishes, the coarser flesh of the carp found little flavor," admitted the Fish Commission in 1904, "and, under the circumstances, it was perhaps but natural that prejudice should arise, especially because the carp was supposed to be injuring the existing fisheries."

But the carp was here to stay, destined for a notable place in American folklife.—*TI*

32. *The Merits of Carp*

ALL ASPECTS CONSIDERED, it probably would have been better had the German carp never been introduced into North America. Still, I think that folk belief makes the carp out to be more of a villain than he is.

Most sport fishermen will tell you that the carp destroys good fishing because it eats vegetation, muddies the water, and gobbles up the young game fish. The truth is that an excess of carp is more a symptom of ecological problems than the cause of them. The greatest cause of turbidity and related water problems in streams such as the Little Cheyenne Creek of my youth is agricultural runoff. It happens that the German carp spread across the United States at the very time when American agriculture was modernizing, commercializing, and intensifying, bringing attendant increases in erosion.

Erosion and carp are concurrent problems, the far greater of which is erosion. Carp just fill the wildlife vacuum created when waters become unsuitable for more sophisticated fish. Modern America is not the first time and place that the carp has been blamed for all sorts of timely evils. Centuries ago the English had a rhyme, "Turkies, carp, hop, pickerel, and beer, / Came into England all in one year."

Another mistaken belief about carp is that they are stupid fish. I will grant that they were pretty easy to catch in Little Cheyenne Creek, but that was because, first, the water was too murky for them to see and, second, there were so many of them in the creek that they were starving. Anyone who observes carp in a clear lake or creek and tries to walk up to them knows that they are wary. They also are sensitive to sound and vibration.

The most pervasive belief about carp, though, is that they are poor eating. When I say that this is a "belief," I don't imply thereby that carp are either good or bad to eat, only that people have opinions about them that are based on hearsay, not experience. Probably the greatest student of carp culture in history (some distinction, that) was a man named Leon J. Cole, who wrote a definitive study on the fish in 1904. Already then he noticed that opinions about carp were shaped by "the repeated hearsay born of suppositions and complete ignorance of the subject or of misinterpreted observations."

Most any fisherman will tell you that carp are no good to eat. The tacky ones illustrate their opinions whenever they catch carp by throwing the fish up the bank to rot in the sun. A charming habit. How many of these people have ever tasted carp?

I have. My reasonable opinion is that carp flesh is edible, but hardly choice. Without special preparation, even disregarding its many bones, carp ranks way below catfish and crappie. I don't say this in condemnation of carp, because black bass are inferior fish for eating, too, and people still think highly of them. What I do mean is that those folks who claim carp are just terrific food are overcompensating for the sake of argument.

Who eats carp, then?—*TI*

33. *Eating Carp*

IT'S UNLIKELY THAT the flesh of the German carp will become a popular food in this country. The sentiment against
it is too strong. How many times have you heard this recipe
for cooking carp?
    First you nail the head of the carp to a pine board.
Then you clean and scale the carp as usual. Leaving the
cleaned carp on the board, you bake it in the oven for an
hour. Then you throw away the carp and eat the board.
    Even if you read a supposedly serious recipe for prepa-
ration of carp in a fish-and-game magazine, the thing
sounds apologetic. You make complicated sauces to dis-
guise the flavor, or you boil the fish to pulp and make
it into carpcakes, or you do something else to make it
unrecognizable.
    (Many publications devote more space to dough bait
recipes for catching carp than to those for cooking carp.
Flour and cornmeal are basic ingredients, but esoteric
folks add things like vanilla, garlic salt, or cinnamon. Dough
bait has as long a history in North America as does the carp
itself. Henry Robinson, the fellow who brought the carp to
New York in the 1830s, said he caught the ones in his
ponds with little pills of rolled-up fresh bread.)
    Culinary use of carp in·North American generally has
been confined to people with some ties of cultural heritage
to the fish and to people of limited income who exploit it as
a cheap source of food. The only people that I can recall
from my youth who ate much carp were blacks from Great
Bend, Kansas. This tendency in taste had nothing to do
with black people, but rather with being from the poor
side of town.
    In the major cities of the northeastern United States,
immigrant Jews long provided a good market for the carp
catches of commercial fishermen. In this case the ties
were those not only of economic class but also of cultural
antecedents.

On the Great Plains today a similar revival of the market for so-called rough fish, such as carp, derives from the migration of Vietnamese to cities in the region. As Vietnamese settled in such cities as Amarillo, Wichita, and Omaha, they sought to maintain their traditional diet, in which fish predominated. As recent immigrants with limited funds, they bought carp. The Vietnamese market for carp intensified as more people of that immigrant nationality followed the relocation of major beef-packing facilities onto the High Plains.

Hence commercial fishing has intensified on the reservoirs of the region. Commercial fishermen legally can harvest only rough fish, mainly carp. From the lakes of south Texas to the Qu'Appelle River of Saskatchewan, these fishermen systematically remove the very fish that sport fishermen want to get rid of. The beauty of this is that controlled commercial fishing not only serves the cultural needs of particular people in the region but also thins the population of fish that other people regard as inferior.

Maybe it takes a century or so for us to begin to see any virtue in such an introduction from abroad as the carp. On the other hand I don't hear anyone saying good things about bindweed, another biological immigrant I will take up in a later chapter.—*TI*

34. *Gophers*

I DO QUITE a bit of folk singing at meetings throughout the plains region, and one of the most popular songs I do is called "Knockin' Around the Yard." Set to an Irish tune, this folk song from the Canadian plains is about a boy who spends his time killing gophers for the bounty on them. "Me overalls are shabby, and I have no shirt at all," the song says, "but I'm going to get a new outfit with me gopher tails this fall."

The reason that people on the southern and central plains like this folk song is that many of them did the same things as the boy in the song—killed gophers (pocket gophers), usually in alfalfa fields, for the bounty. In various county courthouses I have seen records of the bounties paid on gophers and other pests, and lately I have talked with a number of old farmers and county extension agents, veteran gopher killers all.

The problem with gophers was that they threw up fan-shaped mounds of earth from their underground runs in the alfalfa fields. Operators of mowers had to raise their sickles to avoid the mounds, thereby wasting hay.

An old dairyman named Albert Stolfus told me that in order to clear out his fields and to collect ten-cents-per-tail bounties, he used to trap gophers in their runs. He would find a fresh mound, open up the nearby run, set a trap in the run, cover it with a piece of shingle, cover the shingle with earth—and catch a gopher nearly every time.

After counties ceased paying bounties, it was easier to poison gophers than to trap them. A retired county agent named Paul Gwin said that when he was active in extension work—from 1920 on—the common poison was potassium cyanide. He would use a probe to locate a run near a fresh mound and then put a little poison bait in the run.

Another former county agent named C. F. Gladfelter (a younger fellow; he didn't get started in extension work until 1924) had a reputation as an expert in gopher extermination. Gladdy said you could always find the gopher's run about eight inches from its mound. After locating the run with a pipe, he baited it with strychnine grain.

Gladdy also conducted demonstrations on how to kill rats in poultry houses. A farmer named Noble Easter, he said, had a twenty-by-sixty henhouse with hundreds of rats in it. Easter was trying to get rid of them, but with little effect. He would go into the chicken house at night with a club, plug some holes, and kill as many rats as he could, finishing up by lifting the hens off their nests and clubbing the rats that had crawled under the birds to hide.

Still the rodents proliferated—that is, until Gladdy arrived with a cyanide gas gun. He and Easter, after removing the chickens, of course, plugged the foundation with dirt and began gassing under the floorboards. They could hear the rats sneezing inside. Meanwhile, Easter's rat terrier dog got to sniffing around the foundations and keeled over, but they shook a little air into him and he came to again. The treatment was deadly to the rats: Easter counted eighteen victims under just one floorboard.

I don't remember ever having so much trouble with rats around the place in my time. But then Grandpa Isern said that the guinea hens drove the rats away.—*TI*

35. *Urban Gophers*

THANKS TO THE generosity of the Embassy of Canada, I spent a summer month in Saskatchewan looking into several aspects of the history of agriculture in the province, including, much to the amusement of the more traditional scholars there, the history of gopher control. The western Canadian gopher, called the flickertail, is much more pernicious than the pocket gopher of the southern plains. He ranks second only to the grasshopper as an agricultural pest on the Canadian plains.

I am speaking historically here, for nowadays the flickertail is well controlled by poisons and land use. You don't see many gophers along the rural roadside any more. Where you do see them, however, is in the cities.

Having summered twice on the campus of the University of Regina, I came to enjoy watching the playful young gophers and their more prudent parents sporting about the lawns, which are a part of the Wascana Authority lands of the city. Regina, like other western Canadian cities, has an elaborate park system with an artificial lake, manicured grounds, raised flower beds, countless Canadian geese—and a healthy complement of gophers.

I walked into the Wascana Authority office to see who I could talk to about gophers and their habits, and I was lucky enough to find Lorne Scott. Scott is naturalist for the Wascana Authority, president of the Saskatchewan Wildlife Federation, and at heart, still, a farm boy from over at Indian Head.

Out on the farm he feeds the gophers around his house like pets, but on the Wascana grounds they are a problem, Scott says. Until a few years ago the authority was controlling them with strychnine grain, but strychnine is supposed to be restricted to agricultural use, and after one of the geese turned up dead of strychnine poisoning, federal officials made the park people stop using the poison. (Everybody loves the geese, except people who like to go barefoot in the parks.)

Since then, the flickertails have proliferated. In many areas, such as the college campus, it is impossible to put in flower beds because the gophers go through them like scythes. The little animals also have spread out into private lawns and gardens. When it gets hot, they like an occasional drink from a swimming pool.

Affluent urbanites think it's disgusting to fish these dead gophers out of their pools, but sure enough, if the authorities propose to shoot or trap the critters, then the citizenry bubbles over with sympathy for the "cute little gophers."

Utterly lacking in such sympathy are rugby players. The gophers turn the college field into Swiss cheese. You may say that anyone who plays rugby enjoys getting hurt, but the players prefer to inflict the damage on one another rather than suffer it through an ignominious misstep into a gopher hole. When I visited with Scott, he had just hung up the telephone after a call from a rugby player with a broken ankle.

So every morning the groundskeepers go out with wheelbarrows and spades and fill all the holes in the field. Then they leave a barrel of earth and a spade on the sideline so the players can fill holes during warmups. There are plenty to fill, because by game time the gophers have dug out every hole that had been filled during the morning.

It's a terrible nuisance for the gophers, cleaning up after all these people, but they do keep the place nicely watered, and anyway, time doesn't mean much to a gopher.—*TI*

Part Three
PLAIN FARE

DESPITE A DRY SPELL recently, this has been a good year for sweet corn here on the eastern edge of the plains. I'm not much of a gardener, but I do seem to be able to raise corn—if we get enough rain and the grasshoppers leave it alone. (I don't take gardening seriously enough to irrigate or spray.)

As regional food, roasting ears are probably associated more closely with Iowa and Illinois—the Corn Belt—than with the Great Plains. Still, one of the first crops planted by early plains settlers was corn, and I have a feeling that as much corn-on-the-cob is eaten in the plains states as in any other area.

I don't know where or when the practice of eating immature corn originated, but it was unlikely to have been imported from Europe, seeing as how corn itself was native to this continent. Pike tells of receiving a gift of "corn, meat, and grease" from the Osages in 1806, but, given the time of year (late August) and other of his comments about Osage agriculture, this corn was undoubtedly dried. Forty years later, however, Francis Parkman tells of gladly receiving a gift of "an abundance of green corn and vegetables" while visiting the High Plains trading post that later became Pueblo, Colorado. Unlike Parkman, some immigrants to the plains were slow in developing a taste for corn-on-the-cob, or for corn in any other form. The Germans, for instance, considered it *Schweinefutter,* food fit only for pigs.

In my mind, roasting ears are associated with the "food calendar" that operated on our stock ranch in my youth: butcher beef in the winter, plant potatoes on St. Patrick's Day, fry the first chicken (from the baby chicks we had bought back in the winter) by Memorial Day, and harvest the first roasting ears soon after the Fourth of July.

How to eat corn-on-the-cob properly is a real problem
for the etiquette-minded. Does one eat across the cob or go
around it? And how does one apply the butter without
making too much of a mess? I'm told that the polite way is
to butter and eat only two rows of kernels at a time, but
that seems painfully slow, especially since tender young
sweet corn is a sensual pleasure that requires near gluttony
for genuine satisfaction. Let's face it—those people who
think that fried chicken or barbecued ribs have to be eaten
with a knife and fork are going to have real trouble with
roasting ears.

I recently read a newspaper article (by Marian Burros
of the *New York Times*) on how to butter sweet corn. Four
methods were described: rolling the ear in a shallow dish
filled with melted butter, spreading the butter on the ear
with a knife, rolling the ear on a stick of butter, and using a
piece of buttered bread as a brush. Once the butter is
there, salt and pepper are sprinkled on the ear and it is
ready to eat. I had never before heard of using a piece of
bread for buttering corn, and only in the past couple of
years have I encountered the practice of rolling the corn
on a stick of butter. The method I use was my father's: take
a chunk of butter onto the plate, lace it with salt and pepper, mush it all up together with a knife, then spread it
onto the corn.

My grandfather had what seemed to my young eyes
a wonderful way of eating roasting ears. Dadhoy would
butter and salt his corn, then cut it off the ear directly onto
his plate to eat it. I don't remember how old I was before I
realized that the reason he ate corn this way was because he
disliked wearing his false teeth.—*JH*

37. *Hamburgers*

A GOOD HAMBURGER—a really good hamburger—is about
as hard to find today as a black-footed ferret. The se-

riousness of the situation is reflected in the meteoric rise of the McDonald's franchise and its clones. Consider: the first McDonald's hamburgers to invade our region (about a quarter-century ago) were pretty sorry in comparison with other hamburgers then available, but today the McDonald's hamburger, by process of attrition, is one of the better ones around even though it hasn't improved a bit over the years.

The fast-food burger has even invaded many of the local cafés around the plains. It is much easier (and cheaper, I suppose) to slap a prefrozen patty onto the grill than it is to smash out a ball of hamburger with a heavy iron spatula. Beware the perfectly round, perfectly flat hamburger; real hamburger fries up unevenly. Some restaurants even go so far as to call their cheeseburgers "patty melts," admitting, it seems to me, that they contain more soybean than meat.

The hamburger has come a long way from its origins on the steppes of central Asia centuries ago when nomadic horsemen would use slabs of raw meat as saddle blankets all day long, then eat the pulverized and salty stuff raw for supper. The practice of grinding beef and eating it (perhaps as some sort of sausage) supposedly has some connection with Hamburg, Germany, and people were eating something called "hamburger steak" in this country by 1902.

The hamburger first met bun, according to food historians, at the 1904 St. Louis world's fair, while something akin to a hamburger sandwich was served in a Chicago café in 1917. The modern hamburger, however—the fast-food, meal-on-a-bun, buy-'em-here-and-eat-'em-on-the-road-or-at-the-counter-with-a-bowl-of-chili sandwich—is a creation of the Great Plains: Walt Anderson, a Wichita café owner, started his chain of White Castle hamburger stands in 1920.

The hamburger stands that eventually grew out of Anderson's, however, are not all of the budget variety. I recently ate at a place called Longneckers in Wichita where hamburgers come in two sizes, big and huge, with every-

thing imaginable available as toppings. Customers walk
through a line to order, where the first thing to meet the
eye is a glass-enclosed cooler with two or three front quarters of raw beef hanging in full view. The prices for these
super burgers come in the same two sizes. As Charlotte
Thurman of Plainview, Texas, told me concerning the
Fuddruckers hamburger franchise in Lubbock: "They'll
make you a hamburger that costs more than a steak." Fuddruckers, by the way, with dozens of locations in twenty-five
states and three Canadian provinces, seems to be making some inroads against the Hardees and Burger Kings of
the world.

Where do you go for a real hamburger? Sometimes
even the hometown cafés that Tom writes about don't have
the homemade variety. I can't speak for other plains states,
but in Kansas my hometown café (Cassoday) has usually
served real hamburgers. Susie's Chili Parlor in El Dorado
makes a good hamburger (and a big one) right on the
premises. Then there is Salina's Cozy Inn. You can smell
frying onions from blocks away (if you sit at the counter
instead of ordering from the street window, you might
never get the smell out of your clothes, short of burning
them). The hamburgers are small, but they are flavorful,
cheap, and smashed out on the grill right in front of your
eyes. Find a place that does that and you'll enjoy your
lunch.—*JH*

38. *Cafés*

OVER THE PAST few years, in the course of drives to Saskatoon, Lubbock, Garden City, and other such far-flung jew-
els in the Grain Belt, I have logged a lot of miles across flat
country. And although my wife accuses me of being om-
nivorous, I care about finding decent places to eat along
the way. When you travel the so-called Great American
Desert, it's important to find the oases. It's important also

to avoid the tar pits, and so I offer here a few experienced-based hints on how to recognize bad cafés on the plains.

In the first place, avoid any establishment that you have seen advertised on network television. Why put down your money to pay for a Madison Avenue advertising campaign that insults your intelligence and taste? Check out the home businesses, albeit with caution.

Signs are obvious tip-offs. I don't go into any place with a flashing sign that says "Eat" or "Food." Don't those places have proper names? An immediate cause of suspicion, too, is a sign that attempts to limit the clientele of the establishment or its behavior once inside. "No shirt, no shoes, no service," "We reserve the right to refuse service to anyone," and "Salad bar one time through only" are examples of this sort of notice. These make me wonder what kind of sorry folk have been coming in that cause the proprietors to post such signs.

Once you're inside, certain features of the physical layout are significant. If there are video zippo-zappo machines, I leave. If you have to go through the kitchen to get to the rest rooms, I'd rather not. On the other hand, if there is a woven work of art on the wall depicting bulldogs shooting pool and chewing on cigars, this place might be all right.

The food, of course, is the central question, and you don't have to wait until your order arrives to know whether it will be good. Order some coffee and see if you can get cream for it. If, after you insist on cream from a cow, the waitress still gives you only chalk-dust creamer and you stay to eat, then don't say I didn't warn you. Expect instant mashed potatoes and pale margarine with your meal.

Margarine. That reminds me to register here my dissent to the current media blitzes directed against such staples as butter and lard. "No animal fat," they proclaim, as if it were a point of pride. I question whether democracy and free enterprise can long endure in a country where pie crusts are constructed with vegetable shortening.

Back in the café again, be sure to listen as well as look

around. I don't like to hear hollering and talking from the
kitchen; good cooks are soft spoken and single minded.
Neither can I stomach rock music (or whatever contemporary teenage stuff is called) in a café. Rock music has been
proven to sour milk and to turn iceberg lettuce brown
along the edges.

What you hear in a good café is country and western,
circa 1960. And in a real good café, the waitresses hum
along.—*TI*

39. *Beaumont*

UPLAND PLOVERS scurried across the runway as we swung
into the wind and took off in a rented Cessna on an hour's
flight from Emporia to Beaumont, Kansas. I have heard
there is such a thing as a jet set that frequents the fashionable watering holes of America and Europe. I don't expect
ever to join its ranks. But at least now I'm in the prop set. I
have flown to Beaumont just to eat dinner (the meal you
take at noon).

Harold Durst—microbiologist by training, historian by
avocation, a former boss of mine, and a private pilot—was
my entrée into the elite. Our specific destination was the
Beaumont Hotel. The food there is not all that great; I had
a pretty good chicken-fried steak, but I think that the glory
days of the hotel's cuisine are in the past. The point of
going to Beaumont is how you get there. The Beaumont
Hotel is the only fly-in dining establishment I know of.

The town of Beaumont (present population fewer than
one hundred) sprang up in the 1880s along the Frisco Railroad. All that remains today of the town's once-substantial
railroad establishment is the cypress water tower standing
nicely preserved next to the tracks. The hotel also dates
from the early 1880s.

Beaumont acquired far-flung regional connections
through two developments: the cattle-grazing industry,

whereby it became a receiving and shipping point for Texas cattle fattened on Flint Hills grass, and the oil play, which brought an influx of laborers and capitalists from states to the south.

During the 1950s a rancher and pasture man named Clint Squires owned the Beaumont Hotel. Cattlemen looking over their pastures and oilmen checking on their leases frequented the place. Many of them flew themselves or employed private pilots. As longtime hotel employee Audrey McClure recalled the historic moment, "Some rancher from Texas flew up here and landed on Main Street." A county commissioner and pilot for El Dorado, Mac Childs, then talked Squires into opening a pasture east of town as an airstrip. This proved not only convenient but also a good business gimmick. Advertisements in *National Geographic* and *Fortune* and word of mouth soon brought in considerable airborne clientele. Dinner at Beaumont became, for a certain set, a tradition.

A tradition that Harold and I joined, having located the airstrip despite the bluestem grass covering the whitewashed old tires that are supposed to mark it. At the south end of the strip we made a right onto the blacktop (Broadway?) to taxi into town.

At Main you have to stop at the stop sign. I hopped out and shot a photo of Harold duly obeying the traffic ordinances. Then he taxied across into the grassy lot next to the hotel, which an old propeller and a hand-lettered sign nailed to an elm tree designate as "Airplane Parking." For windy days there are tie-downs.

From there you stroll past the spit-and-whittle benches and into where the prop set meets.

For Harold this was the first and last flight to Beaumont. A few months afterward, while doing a few touch-and-go's, he suffered a fatal heart attack at the controls of that same little Cessna. I'm sure glad we got to make that flight together. I'm glad I took that picture at the stop sign, too.—*TI*

40. *Bierocks*

JIM HAS SPECULATED in past writings as to what creature
might be named the official animal of the Great Plains.
Here's a more palatable question: what food might we designate most representative of life on the plains?

I nominate the bierock, or as I sometimes call it, the
German-Russian answer to the burrito. The bierock is a
piece of sweet dough wrapped around a filling of cabbage,
onions, and beef (or whatever else you want to stuff into it)
and baked.

The bierock is a characteristic food of Germans from
Russia on the southern plains from Texas to Kansas. Germans from Russia in the states from Nebraska north con-
sume the same item, but they call it a runsa.

Both names are figments of German-Russian dialect.
"Runsa" is a word for "belly," and so the name presumably
recognizes the resemblance of the food to a stomach. "Bierock" is a word evolved from the Russian *pirogi* or *pirozhki,* a
name for any food consisting of filling stuffed into dough.
This shows that bierocks are not a German food but a Russian food the Germans picked up while living in Russia.

On the Canadian plains, Ukrainian and other Eastern
European immigrants make what they call "piroges." These
are a soft dough stuffed with potatoes and cheese, boiled,
and served with butter, onions, and sour cream. Piroges
and bierocks are akin in name and in general concept, but
the piroges more closely resemble what German-Russian
Mennonites on the southern plains call "verenikas."

Honestly, I never cared much for verenikas. The Mennonites generally fill them with cottage cheese and serve
them with a white gravy, and the whole mess seems to me
about as exciting as a game of checkers. On the other
hand, I have developed a liking for the piroges of the
north. I can eat a pile of them the way they serve them at
the Romanian-Canadian Culture Club of Regina.

There seems to be quite a bit of confusion about bierocks

among plains folk. In the first place, people think they are a German dish, but they aren't; they're Russian. And no two cooks agree on how to spell the name of the item, either. In fact a single cookbook by German-Russian women from western Kansas, *Das Essen Unsrer Leute,* spells it six different ways: bierock, bieroch, beerock, bierack, beruch, and beroak.

To get back to the original question: why the bierock as the representative food of the plains? In a great book of the 1950s, *The Great Plains in Transition,* Carl Kraenzel said that the keys to survival on the plains are mobility, flexibility, and reserves. Kraenzel must have loved bierocks. You can carry them anywhere, stuff them with whatever you have on hand, and save the leftovers to reheat later.

The bierock also has intercontinental tradition going for it. It is, after all, a plains food of two continents.—*TI*

41. *Back for More Bierocks*

HERE IS HOW to make bierocks, the characteristic food of Germans from Russia on the plains. In the first place, the dough is important. Don't listen to anyone who says you can make bierocks with store-bought, refrigerated bread dough.

First prepare your yeast. Put a couple packages of dry yeast and a tablespoon of sugar into a cup of lukewarm water. Let it stand to dissolve. In another bowl mix three-fourths cup sugar and one tablespoon salt into two cups of warm milk (scalded milk, the old recipes say, but that's not necessary anymore). In still another (big) bowl mix four cups flour, two-thirds cup soft lard, and two eggs. Add the contents of the first two bowls to this one and mix it all up. Let this batter stand and rise for a half-hour or so. What you have here is the *Vorteig,* or predough, which is the key to the whole ethnic tradition of bierock making.

Now add four more cups flour, mix, knead, and put

the stuff aside to rise again. Meanwhile, you can get the filling ready. Most people begin by browning some ground
beef in a large pot, add chopped onions, and then put in
chopped cabbage, cooking until the cabbage is sort of
translucent. Seasoning is according to taste, with garlic salt
commonly used. The proportion of ingredients in the filling is open for dispute. A real Rooshian wants more cabbage than anything else.

Also a question is how best to roll or spread out the
dough to receive the filling. I break off a piece the size of a
tennis ball and roll it out. On this I put a large spoonful of
filling. Then I pull the edges of the dough together on top
and squeeze them together. The trick next is to flip the
bierock over onto the baking sheet, so that the edges of the
dough are down.

Bake the bierocks at 350 degrees until they are as brown
as you want them. Mine come out about the size of a brick,
but not quite as hard. Most people make them smaller.

What got me started on this subject of bierocks was
when at a grocery here in Emporia I found plastic-wrapped,
microwaved bierocks for sale. According to the wrappers
they were distributed by Bob and Thelma's Steak House, a
good restaurant near Hoisington, Kansas. They were pretty
bland, mainly because they contained too little cabbage.

A better commercial product comes from a chain of
drive-ins in Nebraska called Runza Drive Inns. This chain,
with headquarters in Lincoln but with drive-ins in towns
throughout Nebraska and parts of Iowa and Kansas, produces a fairly tasty bierock, which it has trademarked, in
the style of the northern plains, as a Runza. The dough is
not quite the right sweetness or texture, though.

Various church groups and other community organizations all over the plains sell bierocks at festivals and on
special occasions. In my old hometown of Ellinwood, the
Lutheran Women's Missionary League sells them each
summer at a local festival. I have a copy of the 1984 report
of their bierock chairwoman. It says the women worked
two days to make 1,189 bierocks containing 150 pounds

cabbage, 100 pounds onions, and just $15.23 worth of beef. Evidently the real Rooshians prevailed in the filling mix, I thought at first, but then some of the women involved explained that the $15.23 was the amount for purchased beef and that other beef was donated.

The only public complaint about the sale was that the 1,189 bierocks sold out too fast. The hoarders got to the sale early and bought them up dozens at a time.—*TI*

42. *Chickens*

I'VE BEEN GIVING quite a few talks lately about the folk life of the plains, particularly about what it was like growing up on a farm or in a small town in the days before electricity, paved highways, and supermarkets made it possible for country people to live like their city neighbors. One of the major differences between urban and rural back then was that the majority of farms and ranches were nearly self-sufficient as far as food was concerned. If you had a big garden (and a root cellar), a few milk cows (and a spring-house), and a bunch of chickens, then about the only staples you had to buy were yeast, flour, salt, and sugar. A couple of hives of bees and a batch of sourdough and even that shopping list could be cut in. half.

This nutritional self-sufficiency, enforced by economic circumstance, was maintained by work that was occasionally hard, often boring, and once in a while exciting. Consider the keeping of chickens. I vaguely recall setting some eggs and watching for them to hatch, but usually we bought live chicks. Each winter Mother would place an order for a couple of hundred (it seemed like three times that many) at a produce house. They would arrive in February or March in large cardboard cartons, round holes for air cut in the sides, and we would then keep them in the brooder house until they were big enough, and the weather warm enough, to run in a pen.

Fried chicken for Decoration Day, along with creamed peas and new potatoes fresh from the garden, was the aim. By the Fourth of July that menu, at the rate of a chicken or two a day, could be getting a little monotonous. By the end of July the surviving chickens were getting close to maturity, so we would have a mass butchering and head for the locker plant with a good supply of winter rations. A couple of the young cockerels might be lucky enough to be chosen for roosters and two or three dozen of the pullets would be kept as replacements for hens getting too old for steady egg laying.

The eggs we didn't eat were taken to a produce house in El Dorado (or Burns or Cottonwood Falls) to sell or to trade for other foodstuffs. (Many rural plains dwellers still go to town to do their "trading," even though they haven't actually bartered produce—or anything else—for a quarter of a century.) My sister and I shared the egg-gathering duties, along with our other chores—milking cows, gathering wood, feeding calves. I invariably got the job of reaching under a setting hen, one that had acquired the nesting urge. A setter gets possessive and mean and will peck fiercely at anyone who tries to get her off the nest. Actually I rather enjoyed outmanuevering a setter, although I didn't let Rita know that. I hate to think of the armloads of wood she carried to the house as payment (blackmail is perhaps too strong a word) for the times I took care of the setters when it was her turn to gather eggs.

Because a setting hen doesn't lay eggs (and will also sit in a nest and keep the layers away), the setters had to be put into what we called the "prisoner's cage," a lath-and-wire enclosure that Dad had made and Mother had named—a verbal ploy (effective) to make the work seem more enjoyable to us kids. The roofed cage, divided into two equal compartments, was about a foot and a half high, three feet wide, and six feet long, with troughs for food and water on each end. It was mounted on posts and stood three or four feet off the ground. There the hens stayed until we found an egg on the wire floor, an egg that won release for all the setters in that compartment.

Handling the setters was part of the fun of keeping chickens, at least for me, while the daily feeding, watering, and egg gathering was the tedium. The annual cleaning of the chicken house was the hard work, but it helped the garden grow.—*JH*

43. *Fried Chicken*

I'VE HEARD LOTS of stories about unpleasant surprises people have had while gathering eggs. I don't believe my sister or I ever found a blacksnake or a rat or any other kind of a varmint in a nest, although the dogs regularly treed skunks, possums, and raccoons in the hedgerow behind the chicken house. Once they even alerted us to a weasel, which had literally sucked the blood out of several old hens. I don't believe we ever lost any chickens to hawks, either, although one did kill a pet pigeon of mine. Nor did coyotes or stray dogs ever wreak much havoc with our chicken flock.

No, most of the chicken deaths on the Flying H were intentional, not accidental, and the end result was fried chicken. Many people rightly associate pan-fried chicken (and mashed potatoes and white gravy) with the South, but this dish is also one of the staples of Great Plains cookery. Getting the chicken from the pen to the pan is an experience I am sure that many readers remember well, although I am afraid that many younger people think that fried chicken spontaneously generates in red-and-white-striped boxes.

We kept a long wire, fastened to a wooden handle on one end with a hook bent into the other, for hooking fryers by the leg. Tom says that his grandmother had a dog trained to go out and catch live chickens, bringing them to her like a setter retrieving a quail. But then Tom also tells about his friend Rollie spearing a dozen ducks on the ramrod of a muzzle-loading shotgun.

Slaughter followed the snaring, and it seems that nearly everyone I talk to had a different way of killing chickens. We placed a hedge branch, about the size of a broom handle, over the chicken's neck, stepped on both ends, and then pulled the head off. Grandmother Hoy had a hatchet and a chunk of firewood with a couple of nails driven into it about an inch apart. The nails would hold the chicken's head while she pulled back on the legs to stretch the neck for chopping. Some people used a large knife instead of a hatchet. Many people would wring the neck, giving it a sharp twist that separated head from body as surely and as quickly as a hatchet.

What happened next is best described by the old folk saying "jumping around like a chicken with its head cut off." The muscle spasms and spurting blood were definitely not for the squeamish. Neither was the scalding. I can still smell the rankness of feathers freshly dipped in steaming hot water and feel the great dank gobs of feathers and down clinging to my hand as I tried to shake them off so I could grab another handful.

Once the chicken was plucked, the body cavity was then cleaned out, the pinfeathers singed, and the bird readied for a final washing before being cut up and put into the skillet. If Grandpa Rice were visiting, we would save the entrails for fish bait. I also remember often opening up the craws to see what treasures the chicken may have ingested; stories of lost diamond rings or rare coins turning up in a chicken's craw were commonplace, but I don't think I ever found anything but sand.

I will admit that picking up a precut fryer at the supermarket is much easier and less sanguinary than raising your own, but, as the saying goes, you get what you pay for. Farm-fresh chicken freshly killed and fried is a rare treat, and getting rarer each year.—JH

44. *Killing Chickens*

JIM HAS MOURNED the rarity of fresh-killed fried chicken
and has cited his recollections of how the birds were dispatched and processed. My mother explains that killing
chickens is a domestic duty abandoned as soon as one's
mother-in-law ceases to insist on it. But a few people still
raise and kill their own, and I think there is a reason that
has more to it than taste.

The same afternoon I flew back from Beuamont with
Harold Durst, my wife and I drove over the Garnett, Kansas, to meet Alvin and Gayle Peters and go with them to the
farm home of his parents, Loyd and Frieda Peters. They
had raised a bunch of fryers from chicks, as they do every
year, and were ready to kill the last nineteen of them.

These folks go about the business in deft style. Alvin,
with a quickness belying his sedentary occupation as a
schoolteacher, catches the birds from the pen and hands
them to Loyd. Loyd drops them into four cones or funnels
mounted on a stand like a sawhorse (the funnels were salvaged from a poultry processing plant that closed), pulls
their heads through the holes in the bottom with a piece of
wire, beheads them with a butcher knife, and leaves them
to bleed. Somebody drops the bled chickens in a pile on
the grass.

Then Loyd shows up with a bucket of hot water and
commences scalding them. Frieda stands in front of a spinning drum powered by an electric motor and fitted with
rubber fingers; the contraption, purchased for two dollars
from a fellow who paid one for it at a sale and then had
second thoughts, looks like the toothed cylinder in a threshing machine. She holds the scalded chickens up to the rubber teeth, and they whip off the feathers in about twenty
seconds.

Next comes an assembly line in the kitchen, with everyone pitching in to pick pinfeathers, nip off feet and wing

tips, draw entrails, split gizzards, ice down the birds, and bag them. Frieda, doing the drawing, obviously is the linchpin in this smooth process. There is a brief debate between Alvin and Loyd as to the depth of cut required to open a gizzard.

All this produces good fryers, fresh birds that once knew the feel of dirt under their claws. But if I were an economist, I would pick this project apart as fast as Frieda's electric plucker. Consider the initial cost of the chicks; the feed; the shelter; the care; the labor in killing and processing; the space in a freezer, maybe rent on a locker. It won't pay out overall, maybe not even the cash costs, not with the cheap fryers available in supermarkets.

What's the point, then? I think it's that Alvin and Gayle spent the evening on the place. Other kids from the family do, too, sometimes just one or two helping out, sometimes everyone within driving distance. Then there's the distribution, whereby each has to stop by and pick up some fryers, and maybe stay around to talk, and maybe weed the garden, and then have some iced tea.

We took home one of the fryers ourselves, but we took home some other things that will stay with us after we've picked over the bones.—*TI*

45. *Lard*

THOSE OF YOU on fat-free diets had best stop reading right here. Just reading this will clog your arteries. I speak here in praise of lard.

Traditional cooks know that there is a concrete reason they prefer lard, or at least used to, for shortening. Lard, because it contains fewer of the harder constituents of fats, has a low melting point and thus is easily handled in making doughs.

A second reason for using lard is aesthetic. You cannot make a pie crust that crumbles and tastes right without lard. Those advertisements for vegetable shortening are shameless lies. Lard also is an essential ingredient in biscuits and is the only acceptable medium in which to fry chicken or chicken-fried steaks. If you don't care about these things, then you deserve what you get.

It is only in recent years we Americans have developed this aversion to lard and other animal fat that television commercials cater to. We used to prize fat as a source of energy. I have in hand a 1916 bulletin of the Department of Agriculture that says, "The ideal diet should contain sufficient quantities of fat and carbohydrates to ensure it the required amount of energy."

This bulletin points out that peoples of both the polar and tropic regions of the globe were heavy consumers of fat. "As everyone knows," it continues, "dwellers in temperate regions use fat in the diet in many ways, which are determined largely by the prevailing food habits and the kinds of fat procurable, and"—here we get to the heart of the matter in regard to modern attitudes—"in quantities which bear a more or less direct relation to the amount of physical work performed." At that time the average quantity of fat eaten was four and a half ounces per person per day. Pencil pushers and TV watchers, however, just can't stomach this stuff.

What provoked this whole discussion was another visit to the Loyd and Frieda Peters farm, where we rendered lard. Rendering is the process by which the water is cooked out of the fat of a hog. (Bear with me, those of you who already know this.) While we cut the fat into small cubes, Loyd pointed out the pieces of leaf lard, the best parts, which come from around the kidneys of the animal. We did the cooking on a gas stove in the garage, stirring once in a while with a stick.

Loyd and Alvin poured the fat from the pot into the lard press. A bit of cloth, held in place by a rubber band, served as a strainer on the spout of the press as the lard ran into cans. Although it was November, Alvin was barefoot, as usual, and I've never seen him move so fast as he did when that rubber band melted and the strainer came off and hot lard started spewing across the floor. Tradition gives way before the mass media and changes in the economy. Not many folks render lard anymore the way the Peters family does. Not many people know what a good pie tastes like, either.—*TI*

46. *Horseradish*

I'M NOT SURE WHY, but every fall I grind horseradish. I have it planted behind my house, and because I ignore it, it flourishes. The foliage is attractive—it looks a lot like a giant dock plant—and digging the roots in the late fall is easy.

But the grinding is a trial. You have to do it outside, because inside, the fumes are insufferable. I clamp a hand meat grinder on a work table, feed in cut-up pieces of horseradish, and keep my face averted as I turn the crank. I understand that some yuppie types use food processors, but I wouldn't know about that. It can't be as much fun.

Home-ground horseradish, packed in vinegar, is potent and much more tasty than anything off the grocery shelf. As do most people, we use it mainly with beef, but it is fresh from the garden just about the time you need it for cold Thanksgiving-turkey sandwiches. Best of all is to roll up the fresh stuff undiluted into slices of dried beef from some such outstanding butcher shop as the Burdick (Kansas) Locker. Don't breathe out your nose when it's in your mouth.

Horseradish is a root crop well adapted to the Great Plains and is commonly raised in the region. Once you become aware of it, you spot patches of it in yards all over the town and country. Horseradish is not picky about the soil it will grow in, but the humus-rich, generally clay-free soils found through most of the plains are ideal for it. On the

High Plains it needs watering during the summer. Hardly any bugs will touch it.

As best I can tell, the coming of horseradish to the plains went largely unrecorded by scribes, but from agricultural bulletins I've read, I do know that at the turn of the century the use of horseradish as a relish had become something of a culinary fad across the country. I suspect that both Anglo-Americans and Europeans brought the plant to the plains before that. Through generations and migrations it has been passed along by cuttings in true folklorish fashion. I got my cuttings from a Flint Hills upland farm woman named Enola Brown.

Now maybe I've touched on the mystery of my first line: why I grind horseradish. Still I suspect there is more to it than love of folklore. A Department of Agriculture bulletin from 1916 tells me that horseradish is in my blood (that blood all being of Hanoverian German derivation).

"A very palatable sauce is made as follows," it says. "Thicken milk with cracker crumbs by heating them together in a double boiler, using 3 tablespoons of cracker crumbs to 1½ cups of milk. Add ⅓ of a cup of grated horse-radish, 3 tablespoonfuls of butter, and ½ teaspoonful of salt; or thicken with butter and flour some of the water in which the meat was boiled, add a generous quantity (1 or 2 tablespoonfuls) of grated horseradish, boil a short time, and serve. This recipe is the most usual in German homes where the sauce is a favorite."

The report from trials in my own laboratory is that if you cream horseradish like this, it loses potency and you need to grate in a little raw stuff just before serving.—*TI*

47. *Sandhill Plums*

I GREW UP in the close vicinity of Plum Buttes, a nooning site just past Cow Creek crossing on the old Santa Fe Trail.

From here southwestern travelers got their first glimpse of the sandy, treeless ribbon that was the Arkansas River of the early nineteenth century, not the smelly, scrubby trickle of today. Plum bushes still grow in the sandy pastures around here, and to them, on July 4, 1986, my wife and I repaired to pick a batch of sandhill plums. The historical precedent in this ritual seemed appropriately patriotic for the holiday, and besides, sandhill plum is the best jelly there is (next to rose hip). The jelly my spouse produced from those Independence Day plums was a beautiful, clear, state-fair red.

The sandhill plum (also called Chickasaw plum), *Prunus angustifolia,* is one of those regional legacies that we of the southern and central Great Plains can enjoy the same as did our forebears. The very first Europeans to traipse across this country noted these plums with relish. The fellow who took the official notes on the Coronado expedition of 1540–41, Pedro de Castañeda, thought the countryside "very similar to that of Spain," with "plums like those of Castile."

Another writer with the same outfit, Juan de Jaramillo, agreed: "We found plums, of a variety not exactly red, but shading off from reddish to green," he said. "The tree and its fruit are surely Castilian, the plums being of excellent flavor."

Castañeda and Jaramillo were writing about the place called Quivira, which is Rice County, Kansas, which is Plum Buttes. Take a look at this jelly, Pedro.

Among the most perceptive of the Anglo-American explorers of the southern plains, George C. Sibley liked the sandhill plums, too. Riding through the sandhills of northwestern Oklahoma in 1811, he noted the "thickets of dwarf plumb bushes not over thirty inches in height from which we gathered a great abundance of the most delicious plumbs I ever tasted."

Later settlers of the region stretching from Texas to Nebraska knew the same plums and plucked them from the same thickets. There are wild plums throughout the temperate parts of North America, but surely none were so cherished by pioneers as were these sandhill plums. Other wild fruits, or at least familiar ones, were scarce on the plains, and domestic fruits brought out by the pioneers did poorly. Sandhill plums filled the fruit gap in the pioneer diet.

As did my ancestors, I picked sandhill plums as a boy. I also discovered that during the snowy stretches of winter, you could always find cottontails, and often a rooster pheasant, in the thickets, prime cover for all sorts of wildlife.

Only years later, after having lived elsewhere long enough to develop a higher appreciation of homely delicacies, did I notice the pale plum blossoms that annually adorned the pastures and roadsides. And only recently have I recognized how much more important the plums were to the pioneers than they are to us, who use them only for jelly and jam.—*TI*

48. *Plum of the Pioneers*

TO PIONEER WOMEN of the southern plains, sandhill plums were much more than the stuff of jelly and jam to show off at the fair. Commonly they canned many quarts of the little fruits. Nineteenth-century canners heated them in the open kettle, but their daughters converted to the radical new cold-pack method.

Canned or fresh the plums went into pies and cobblers or frequently appeared on the table just stewed. The cook herself might be wearing an apron dyed with plum juice. Cotton cloth colored with plum juice could be set with vinegar.

I have in hand now a sample of such work, a cloth dyed by Norma McMillan of Stafford County, Kansas. (Norma has been doing local research on folk use of sandhill plums, which abound in her vicinity.) The cotton cloth has taken on a fetching shade of lavender, whereas I would have expected it to be peach or pink.

None of this is to deny that sandhill plums are at their best as jelly and butter. An important consideration for earlier generations, before commercial pectin, was that the plums would jell. Their acidic sourness was a virtue in this regard. The plums, like many other fruits, jelled best if not dead ripe. Good plum juice would jell nicely with equal parts of sugar.

After the juice was extracted for jelly (or dye), the pulp could be run through a colander and made into plum butter. This was the prudent thing to do with dead-ripe fruit, too, unless you had plenty of time to waste waiting to see if the juice would jell. Another reason for making butter instead of jelly was that it took less sugar, which was a consideration both during pioneer times and during the world wars.

Sandhill plum butter is not too popular these days. I think the reason that sandhill plum jelly remains a favorite, in the home and at the fair, is that it's so pretty. No other jelly looks so warm on the shelf or glows so cheerily in the sunlight. The taste is delicate, but not bland like domestic plum.

Sandhill plums also had other than culinary value to the pioneer community. As Norma McMillan writes, "The gathering of the fruit became a social event. Many times several pioneer neighbors would gather together to pick plums. The children were always taken along to gather the dead branches for use as kindling or firewood. This was a time of catching up on the news, and each woman tried to out-do the others with the clarity and beauty of the canned fruit, jellies, and jams."

Could this tradition revive? I doubt it, even with Sure-Jell. The sticking point is the picking. Sandhill plum thickets are neither as prickly as gooseberries nor as chiggery as elderberries, but they have some thorns, all right. The thickets thrive, too, in the same sort of sandy areas as do Mexican sandburs. And rattlesnakes.

Besides, it's mighty hot out here at Plum Buttes on the Fourth of July. How far is it to the windmill?—*TI*

49. *Schwatzberra*

HERE IS A BIT of Great Plains plant culture that has the botanists confused. There is an American nightshade plant, *Solanum ptycanthum*, native to the plains from Texas to North Dakota. People consider it poisonous. It is, I am pretty sure, the same species as the Eurasian nightshade, *Solanum interius*, which is commonly consumed by humans.

What makes all this tricky is that during the 1870s Germans from Russia brought Eurasian nightshade seeds to the American plains, and they called the berries *Schwarzbeeren*, or as they pronounced it, *Schwatzberra*, which means "blackberries."

Germans from Russia on the plains still raise these Schwatzberra and consider the pastries they make from them a highlight of their culinary culture. The ripe berries are purple and small, just a little bigger than elderberries. The plants they grow on are not woody bushes like blackberry bushes but annual plants with a taproot. You can start them from seed, and in a couple of years they try to take over your yard.

I had the chance to sample a variety of Schwatzberra pastries baked by Alma Herl, a Volga German native of Ellis County, Kansas, now living in Halstead, Kansas, which is Mennonite country. She had Schwatzberrakuchen, Maultaschen, and pies. She also had a sample of the seeds, which look like tiny tomato seeds.

Germans don't make pies, but the Germans from Russia learned to make them after they arrived on the American plains, and so they put their berries into the new pastry and had Schwatzberra pies. More traditionally they continued making Schwatzberrakuchen, or cakes, but these aren't like the cakes of Anglo-Americans. These Kuchen

begin with a yeast dough, like a bierock dough, on which
you spread stewed and sweetened Schwatzberra. Atop this
you sprinkle Grimmel, that is, a crumb topping made of
flour, sugar, and butter.

Maultaschen, sometimes called Seckel (meaning "pock-
ets"), are similar to turnovers. The turnover-pockets are
formed of the same sort of yeast dough and filled with the
same sweetened Schwatzberra. Then you either boil them,
schmelz (sauté) them with butter, and serve them with cream
or top them with Grimmel and bake them.

If a non-German-from-Russia bites into one of these
pastries expecting to taste something like American blackberries, he is in for a surprise. Schwatzberra have none of
the tartness of other common berries. They may be sug-
ared up, but always in there is the faint bitterness characteristic of nightshade plants. Food is culture, of course, and
generally German-Russians like the taste, but other folk
are queasy about it. The taste of Schwatzberra reminds me
of the saskatoon berry, which Canadian plainsmen make
into pies. (They served saskatoon pie in the Saskatchewan
pavilion at the 1986 Vancouver Expo.)

Although some people have digestion problems with
Schwatzberra, the ripe, purple berries are not poisonous.
They are, however, a tedious chore to pick.—*TI*

50. *Mulberries*

IT'S STRANGE THAT although countless plains folk have
fond memories associated with mulberry trees from child-
hood, they complain about them as adults. They come to
disdain the fruit for eating. (I disagree, as I'll show later.)

And they cite many other trivial problems. The juicy
fruit, they say, leaves indelible stains, especially after going
through fruit-eating birds. Mulberry stains used to deco-
rate laundry on lines; now they grace the finish of auto-

mobiles. In the yard mulberries make a sticky mess on the ground and attract flies.

Complain if you want to, but people brought mulberries out to this section of the country for good reasons. In the first place, nineteenth-century settlers believed that the plains states were destined to develop a great silk industry. State governments voted bounties to encourage their hopes. That silk from the plains states eventually proved uncompetitive in the international market does not mean that early hopes for it were silly. (By that standard the oil industry would be silly, too.)

So the silk promoters brought out mulberry trees, as did many other settlers who planted them for their own reasons. They planted the Russian variety, *Morus alba,* which may be either black or white. The native American red mulberry, *Morus rubra,* is not hardy enough for the plains. German-Russian Mennonites claim credit for introducing the Russian mulberry, and they undoubtedly did so, but so did many other settlers.

The great virtue of *Morus alba* is ability to survive. "It is one of the hardiest trees planted on the Plains," observed the assistant forester of the United States in 1909, "and serves a number of useful purposes. . . . The Russian mulberry grows quite rapidly, and endures almost any amount of drought and neglect."

Mulberries thus were a common resort for hedgerows, shelterbelts, and even clipped hedges. The courthouse grounds in Phillipsburg, Kansas, showcased a fine grove of mulberries planted in 1883. A beautiful stand of two hundred mulberries planted in 1893 at Ashland, Kansas, was pictured in a U.S. Forest Service circular in 1909.

A Forest Service bulletin of 1911 further noted, "The Russian mulberry has been planted extensively in Nebraska and Kansas, and on account of its very vigorous and rapid growth yields a good revenue from posts at an early age." The mulberry is of the same genus as the Osage orange and produced posts almost as durable. Its habit of

sprouting suckers from roots and stumps made it all the
more prolific in producing valuable posts. Mulberry logs
were good, hot fuel, too.

Once introduced to the plains, mulberries spread readily. Birds and animals dropped the seeds everywhere. They
sprouted and survived in fencerows and other unculti-
vated places, but did best along streams. And they spread
the better along streams because the fruits floated.

People on the plains past were loath to waste all this
readily available fruit. Since the trees and berries are still
with us, why not take a look back at how they may be
used?—*TI*

51. *Mulberry Pie*

I PICKED MULBERRIES every year when I was a kid. They
ripened just before harvest, and I tried not to knock down
too much wheat walking out to lonely trees along quarter-
section lines. Generally I went barefoot and had purple
feet for a week afterward.

Some years, when we wanted berries in quantity, we
gave up hand picking and instead shook them down. Ripe
berries fell readily onto sheets of plastic spread beneath
the branches.

The berries all went into pies. I just don't understand
people who turn up their noses at mulberry pie.

Admittedly, the flavor of mulberries does not stand
alone well. They are sicky-sweet and otherwise bland. They
should be mixed with some other filling, something tart.

Rhubarb makes a good mix. I rustled enough berries
for a couple of pies this summer, and we mixed them with
rhubarb. (Under a lard crust, of course.)

Before I got old enough to like rhubarb, my mother
mixed mulberries with pie cherries, which also makes a
fine pie. Tart cherries ripen at about the same time as
mulberries.

The most interesting mixer, however, is gooseberries, preferably wild ones. I'm not chemist enough to say why, but when you mix gooseberry and mulberry, the resulting pie is remarkably like boysenberry.

The last mulberry pie I ate came from my mother, and I was sorry to see that the mulberries in it were unstemmed. I stem them. To do this best, you need to arrange your bowls conveniently, then go to work with scissors. My research shows that it takes eight minutes and thirty seconds to stem a heaping cupful, which means that it takes seventeen minutes to stem enough for mixing in a pie.

Meanwhile, you think about the tradition of which you are a part. Thrift, self-sufficiency, and all those other pioneer virtues. A Mennonite friend of mine, Leann Toews, writes: "Mennonites were and still tend to be frugal. The mulberry tree was not wasted. . . . Even though it did not work out for silk, it provided jars and jars of jam for the winter and many pies were made to feed hungry threshing crews. Today there is not a pot luck in Goessel [Kansas] where one can't find a mulberry-currant, mulberry-rhubarb, mulberry-cherry, or plain mulberry pie."

Let me add one final point in praise of mulberries, something we on the plains generally overlook when we cuss the mess made by berry-gorged birds. Birds prefer mulberries to all other early-season fruits. In other parts of the country, keepers of orchards, particularly cherry orchards, commonly planted groves of mulberries nearby to decoy the birds.

So, unawares, we in this section of the country get one more culinary benefit from mulberries. Even people who don't want to eat mulberries have their preferred domestic fruits at least partly saved from birds by the presence of wild-growing mulberries in the region.—*TI*

Part Four

PLAYING GAMES

ONE OF MY FAVORITE games when I was growing up was shinny. For those who have never played, it's a bit like ice hockey, only played on solid earth and without nets or definite numbers of players or playing positions. Players hit a puck with a stick, trying to get it over a goal line in order to score. There is no goalie, however, to help keep the puck from crossing the score line. Actually there is no puck either. Instead the game begins with an empty tomato or pork-and-beans can, which after a half-hour or so of hard play gets transformed into a ball-shaped projectile capable of great speed, distance, and impact.

A good shinny stick is not easily acquired, for most of them resulted from many exploratory trips to the timber, looking for a stick of just the right size with a curve of just the right angle. Occasionally a good stick could be rescued from the pile of firewood being sawed for winter. The general shape and length is that of a golf club: straight shank with an L-shaped foot extending about four inches at about a hundred-degree angle. The stick needs spring and some heft but shouldn't be too big around or too heavy. Hickory made good shinny sticks, and so did hedge.

Our playing fields often had no side boundaries, just goal lines, so the game stopped for nothing except exhaustion—or injuries. We had no referees because there were few rules and the game tended to police itself. The only real rule, as I remember, was "shinny on your own side," which meant that you had to hit the can right-handed toward your goal, even if you were left-handed. If you were hitting from the wrong side (which was tempting to do if you were racing down the field after the can and trying to get it back toward your goal before an opposing player, already on the correct side, could hit it), then you were open for a legal crack across the shins. Many other such hits took place, all purported to be accidental. Some probably were.

There was a ritual to start the game or begin play after each goal. Two opposing players would set the can up in the center of the field and then chant simultaneously, "One, two, three," touching the ground with their sticks then raising and touching them just above the can on each count. After touching sticks on the last count, you were free to slam the can. You could, however, try a little finesse and plant your stick hard on the ground in front of the can just as the other player swung, a manuever that not only left you with a good open shot but also sent a tooth-jarring shock all the way up the arms of your opponent.

We played shinny mostly in the cow pastures at home. I do remember one time playing at school, but after about the second day of this recess mayhem we were told to take our shinny sticks home and leave them there. Shinny was one of the standard recess games in my father's generation, however, and he says that shinny sticks stacked in the hallway were as common as coats and hats. I think, from the stories I have heard from that day and age, that the teachers were probably glad to have the students expend as much energy as possible during recess, even at the expense of a few cracked shins.—*JH*

53. *More Shinny*

IN THE LAST CHAPTER I wrote about shinny, the wild and sometimes painful game that resembles hockey only played on land and with a tin can for a puck. A straight piece of hedge or hickory with a short "foot" curving out on the bottom end made the best shinny sticks, and the object was to knock the can across the goal line of the opposing team. Instead of being called "field hockey," the game was termed "shinny" because of the regularity with which the sticks seemed to come in contact with the lower leg.

Most shinny sticks were homemade, cut during a special trip to the timber or else rescued from a piece of wood destined for the woodpile. My father tells of one boy, whose family was apparently a bit more well off than some, who brought a brand new, brightly painted, store-bought shinny stick to school at Cassoday one day. His shins were so tattooed by the end of the day that he never brought it back.

Recently I learned from Joe Davis of Plainview, Texas, of a variation of shinny he played back in the 1920s. Mr. Davis attended Liberty School about five miles north of Plainview, a rural school but a fairly large one—four rooms with an auditorium and basketball court later added on, a peak enrollment of 126 in the early 1930s. The games played there were similar to those played in other schools across the Great Plains: basketball, baseball (called "town ball," perhaps from town-team baseball), marbles, and leapfrog (called "one-and-over").

Unlike town ball and one-and-over, which have variant names for relatively standard games, Liberty School shinny had an entirely different configuration from any other version of that game that I have heard of. As you will see, it was an odd-man-out game, sort of a roughhouse version of musical chairs. Only half a dozen boys could play at any one time (Davis doesn't recall any girls ever playing), and it was an individual, not a team, sport. Some five shallow, plate-size depressions (the "bases"), about six or eight feet apart, were circled around a center hole. Players used straight sticks and a tin can.

One boy, the "it," was stationed outside the ring while five other boys guarded each of the peripheral holes. The "it" would hit the can toward the center hole while the defenders would try to knock the can away. The object, however, was not to get the can in the center hole but for the "it" to try to capture one of the peripheral holes. If he could drive the can past the ring of defenders, the "it" would force one or more of them toward the center and away from a base, thus leaving it open for capture. Once a base was captured, that boy became "it" and had to go to the outside position.

No score was kept (in fact, points weren't possible), and the game had no defined ending. You just played, Davis said, until "the teacher came out with the old hand bell ringing for 'books.'" While quite different in many respects from Cassoday shinny, the Liberty version did share two common elements. Again from Mr. Davis: "Yes, there were some sore shins, but it was fun."—*JH*

54. *Prairie Polo*

NOT TOO LONG AGO I read a news item about the formation of a professional polo league, a faster indoor game with three players per team instead of the usual four. The gist of the article was that polo was attempting to shed its aristocratic image and become a sport that would attract proletarian spectators. What many people don't know is that up until the Second World War, polo was common on the central plains, and plainsmen are about as democratic as you could want.

Bob Frizzell of Larned, Kansas, played polo in the 1930s for New Mexico Military Institute, a real hotbed of polo activity. One of the top college teams of that time, Arizona University, was fed by NMMI graduates, according to Frizzell. New Mexico's Springer Ranch provided many good mounts for NMMI, a cavalry school, but when some of the players began to bring in hot-blooded horses, Frizzell said, the game got a little too dangerous. The high-strung horses would go all out for the ball, and many wrecks and serious injuries resulted.

During roughly the same time period, St. Joseph's Academy in Hays, Kansas, held polo matches on its grounds. One of the most successful polo teams in the Hays area in the 1930s was composed entirely of members of the Philip family. Doug Philip's grandfather came over from Scotland in the mid-1870s to work for George Grant, founder of the model farm set up for English gentry at Victoria (and thus,

I would guess, the possible site of some early polo matches on the plains). After the Victoria experiment failed, the Philip family put together a couple of large ranches and raised some top Herefords for many years—in addition to playing polo.

Doug Philip said that the earliest polo team he remembers was one that Ralph Bowlby had in the 1920s. These players used a combination of equipment—"pancake" saddles and helmets along with Levi's and cowboy boots—to play polo on the prairie. Bowlby's ranch was in northeast Ellis County, and he and his teammates would often ride thirty or forty miles on a Sunday, play polo, then ride back home. Russ Townley of Russell, Kansas, recently told me that he remembers polo teams from Gorham and Natoma playing in some sort of league as late as 1947–48.

Polo was also played in the tallgrass region. Dick and Punk Kimbell, for instance, had a polo team on their ranch near Virgil, Kansas. And my father and uncle still have the mallets they used for Sunday afternoon games when they were in high school. Glen Watkins, who lived east of Cassoday, was one of the organizers of the games there.

When the Santa Fe completed its tracks through Cassoday in 1923, Watkins sponsored a big celebration—two days of barbecue, dancing, rodeo, and polo. A team from Wichita was invited to provide competition, and the surviving photographs of the two opposing teams are a study in contrasts. The Wichita foursome look like pros—helmets, jodhpurs, high-topped English riding boots, two-bitted and four-reined Pelham bridles, English saddles (what my father calls "riding a postage stamp")—while the Cassoday players look like what they are: working cowboys. They are dressed in hats and boots and are sitting their cow ponies in regular stock saddles.

The Wichita team won the first match because their horses went right after the ball and the cow horses, trained not to get hit by angry bulls or kicking horses, dodged out of the way. That night the Cassoday team decided that for the next game they would hold their horses on the ball, no matter what. The next day when two horses went charging after the polo ball and met in a thunderous crash, you can guess which player went flying through the air—it sure wasn't the experienced bronc rider in his high-backed, wide-swelled stock saddle.

So the Cassoday team was vindicated in the second game. For some reason the Wichita team turned down a third game to play off the tie.—*JH*

55. *Donkey Ball Games*

I DON'T THINK I have seen a poster for a donkey ball game for years. Are they still being held? I remember very clearly the donkey basketball game held in the Cassoday High School gym; it must have been around 1950, maybe earlier. I know that I was still in grade school because, as a preliminary event, there was a race on wooden donkeys for grade-school students. I won the race and I can still see that crisp, clean, new dollar bill that was first prize.

I don't remember much about the game itself or about the occasional donkey baseball (actually softball) games that were played on the grade-school diamond, except that watching grown men try to play ball from the backs of contrary burros was hilarious. Recently I visited with Emporian Ken Scott, who was a donkey softball entrepreneur back in the Depression.

In 1933 Scott had just graduated from college and was, he said, like everyone else at that time, looking for anything that could make a few dollars. He read in *Billboard* magazine about a promoter from Texas who was touring the big eastern cities with donkey ball games, so Scott and a partner got a livestock commission man (who did a lot of traveling in the Southwest) to locate ten burros (at twenty-five dollars each) and ship them to Emporia. The burros, some bridles, a rented truck, and a road manager comprised the total investment.

Scott himself went on the road (Kansas, Missouri, Nebraska, Iowa, Minnesota, the Dakotas) to line up playing dates. From April to September the donkeys were earning their keep some five or six nights a week—and making a decent profit for their owners in the process. Scott would get a couple of local service organizations (Rotary, Lions, etc.) to sponsor a contest. The local people took care of promotion, and the gate proceeds were split evenly. A good day could bring in over two hundred dollars free and clear to each side.

The money was so good, in fact, that Scott could afford to get married. He continued with the business for about four years, then sold out to his partner, who kept it going through the end of the decade.

The major attraction of a donkey ball game is seeing local citizens, often business and professional people, getting thrown off and stepped on by contrary donkeys. There were several broken bones and lots of bruises, Scott told me, but no lawsuits. One genuine backwoods Missourian, angry at being continually tossed, took after his mount with a knife but was stopped before he could inflict any serious damage.

Not long ago I was talking to Bert Lewis of Kinsley, Kansas. During the 1930s he and his brother, who still ranch between Kinsley and Dodge City, wintered some donkeys for a donkey ball team (not Scott's). There were about a dozen donkeys, he told me, and before the winter was over they had given each one of them a name—names like Mae West, Jack Dempsey, King Kong. The next spring Lewis learned that they had given about a fourth of the donkeys the very same names that the owners had given them, including Mae West.

I asked Scott if they had named their donkeys. "Yes," he said, "but I don't remember any of the names, except for Mae West." Poor Mae. Sex goddess of the 1930s and namesake of a burro in every donkey ball team in the plains.—*JH*

56. *Bullfighting on the Plains*

I WAS RECENTLY reading the *Personal Narrative* of James Ohio Pattie, an account of a young Missourian's journey through the Great Plains and his five-year sojourn as a trapper (and prisoner) in the Spanish Southwest of the 1820s. It's a fascinating account, filled with details of Indian fights, buffalo hunts, and grizzly bears. One thing I was especially looking for in the story was evidence of early rodeolike activities at the fiestas and missions. There were a few tantalizing references to the roping and riding skills of the vaqueros, but the only organized sports that Pattie described in any detail were bullfights.

One, in California, pitted fighting bulls against grizzlies; something like fourteen bulls were required to kill the five bears released one at a time into the arena. A bull's first charge and hook at the bear was usually his best—and last—shot. If he missed, the grizzly more often than not dispatched him with one powerful blow.

Pattie briefly describes another bullfight in Mexico City, the standard sort of spectacle of matador versus *toro*. The first bullfight he saw, however, was closer to the plains. It occurred in New Mexico shortly after his party had arrived in Santa Fe. Here the *banderillas* (the barbed sticks shoved into the bull's neck to weaken the muscles that hold the head erect) were filled with gunpowder. Once all were in place, one of the *toreros* created a fireworks display by passing a torch over the back of the bull as he charged by.

There may have been others, but the one genuine American Great Plains bullfight that I know of took place in Dodge City in 1884. There, as part of a Fourth of July celebration that included horse races, baseball games, and a roping contest, a troupe of Mexican bullfighters fought and killed several Spanish fighting bulls despite a public outcry from the eastern part of the state. Another bullfight was held in Dodge City in 1984 to mark the centennial of the original, but this time, as I understand it, the bulls were fought from horseback in the fashion of the French Camargue region—that is, they were not killed.

The Camargue is a French version of the Great Plains (only much smaller), a flat, grassy, stock-raising area along the lower Rhone that has a tradition of animal sports—roping and throwing cattle—analogous to rodeo. The Camargue, in addition to its regular horseback bullfights, is also home to some of the wildest variations of man versus bull ever dreamed up, according to a Calvin Trillin article I read in the *New Yorker* during the winter of 1984.

In *taureaux piscine* (which means literally "bull swimming pool"), a score or so of young men are in an enclosed arena with a plastic swimming pool (a small backyard wading pool) and a bull. The first person to be in the pool simultaneously with the bull wins the money. Then there is *taureaux pasteque* ("bull watermelon"), in which the first person to finish eating a slice of watermelon wins the prize. The complication is that the contestant cannot take a bite of melon unless he is sitting on a bench—a bench placed in the middle of a bullring complete with fighting bull. Finally, there is *taureaux football*, a standard soccer game following all the standard soccer rules, except that there is a snorting bull running loose in the playing field.

I'm not about to speculate on all the sociological implications, but it is interesting to note the way in which different nationalities have responded to the mythic power of bulls: the French play games among them, the Spanish fight them to the death, and the Americans ride them.—*JH*

57. *The Eskridge Rodeo*

FOR OVER THIRTY YEARS the small town of Eskridge, Kansas, on the eastern edge of the Flint Hills has held a two-performance rodeo on Labor Day (one show in the afternoon, one in the evening) with a barbecue (free to rodeogoers in preinflationary times) held between performances. Eskridge had a rodeo again this year (1985), its thirty-third, but it was professional (i.e., sanctioned by the redundantly titled Professional Rodeo Cowboys Association) instead of the open-to-the-world (i.e., "amateur" in rodeo parlance, even though entry fees are charged and prize money given) contests that obtained until this year, and it was held on two days: Sunday and Labor Day. In previous years Eskridge often drew cowboys from as far as Texas and the Dakotas, although most of the contestants were from Kansas and the hometown or surrounding counties.

Some of these local boys were good (I know of at least four Eskridge competitors who later won world championships in the RCA—oops, the PRCA), but the overall flavor of Eskridge was that of a cattle-country folk festival: local cowboys getting together to see who could rope fastest or ride best. That's how rodeo started, and that was the tradition that Eskridge helped to maintain.

Professional rodeo cowboys are skilled, but their competitive performances have a slickness, a lack of the spontaneity that is found in the best of the amateur rodeos. It's a little like comparing professional football with college football. Both games are good, but for different reasons. The pros are smooth, impressive—and predictable. A Cowboys game (or a Raiders game, or whichever) is like a Holiday Inn: no surprises. With college ball, however, there is less awesome display of power and skill but more enthusiasm, excitement, and razzle-dazzle.

Another reason I hated to see Eskridge change was because it was one of the first rodeos in which I ever competed. I was around fifteen years old and wanted to be a calf roper, like my Uncle Marshall, and had been doing a little practicing on the bucket calves at home. I had achieved my full height (six feet) at that age, but was otherwise not full grown; I doubt if there were more than 140 pounds on my skinny frame.

The calves at Eskridge that year were pasture-fat Angus that were big bodied and short legged and must have weighed nearly four hundred pounds—at least they looked that big on the end of a rope. I don't think I ever got out on a calf better or roped one quicker than I did that afternoon, but I spent the next two minutes (it seemed longer, much longer) just trying to leg that calf to the ground so that I could tie it. Eddie VanPatten and Bob Widau (two top ropers and bulldoggers who were ramrodding their hometown rodeo in the mid-1950s) finally came out and helped me get the calf down. I was disqualified, of course, but by then it didn't matter.

The bad thing was that I knew I had another calf during the night performance. I didn't really want to, but I caught the second calf just as quickly as I had the first one. Even all that free barbecue between shows hadn't helped me. It was more than a little humiliating to a teenager, but Eddie and Bob had to come to my rescue again.

My son and I went to the Eskridge rodeo this year, despite the changeover, and I'm happy to report that it has kept its aura of genuine cow-country contest. Not only were there enough professionals from this area to help retain the local flavor, but the Eskridge promoters kept the wild-cow-milking contest. No matter who enters one of those—professionals or local ranch hands—a wild-cow milking is going to evoke the flavor of an old-time rodeo.—JH

58. Tame Buckers

RECENTLY A MAN came up after a rodeo-history program I had given and told me about an unusual bucking horse he had seen as a boy at a rodeo near Elida, New Mexico. The horse was a buckskin owned by Harold Crosby, who rode him to help pen cattle, then rode him around the arena a couple of times. At that point they took the saddle off the horse, put a loose rope around him in a bucking chute, and a cowboy attempted to ride him bareback. The horse threw the rider high into the air, shook off the rope, jumped the arena fence, and headed for the Crosby ranch at Kenna a few miles away, jumping fences to get there. He had been taught that he could go home once he had bucked off a bareback rider.

Many people think that rodeo bucking horses are wild, but often just the opposite is true. In fact, many of the best buckers are former saddle horses that simply obeyed their bucking instinct and found that they liked it. But they are still tame and gentle to handle, and some of them can continue to be ridden as regular riding horses.

I remember from my own youth a horse named Sambo that Wilbur Countryman bucked as a saddle bronc at his annual Fourth of July rodeo—after the horse had been ridden to round up the bucking stock and maybe even had some calves roped off him. I also remember a bareback bronc Floyd Rumford had in his string, a horse named Dangerous Dan. After he had made his trip into the arena from the bucking chutes, usually throwing his rider, he would be caught and saddled by the pickup men and a small child would crawl around his legs, then get on him and ride him out of the arena.

Recently I talked to Floyd's son Bronc, who had just roped a calf at the Flint Hills Rodeo in Strong City, Kansas. The horse he was riding, a seven-year-old quarter-horse gelding named Bar, can be used for about anything. Bronc hazed about half the steers in the bulldogging contest that afternoon on him, and he told me that his young daughter often used Bar in the barrel race. The only problem with the horse is that he takes about twenty minutes to warm up each day he is ridden. During those first twenty minutes he can buck like a fiend if he gets his head down.

About three years ago at a college rodeo produced by the Rumford Rodeo Company, Bronc noticed a new horse, Bar 100, listed in the bareback draw. When he got back to his horse trailer, he saw a paint brand on the horse he had roped twenty head of calves on that day. He had also hazed several bulldogging steers and helped sort and move stock. But when the chute gate opened in the bareback riding that evening, Bar 100 threw his rider quickly. In fact, Bronc told me, Bar is undefeated, having thrown six cowboys in his six trips into the arena as a bucking horse. He is a well-made horse, full of muscle with a bright eye and a nice disposition. Someone once asked Bronc why anyone would take a chance of ruining a good calf-roping horse by bucking it. His answer was that if it came to that the horse would have an easier life as a bronc and would actually be worth more to Rumford Rodeo as a bucking horse than as a using horse.—*JH*

59. *Pretty Prairie*

IN ALL THE United States and Canada there is only one town called Pretty Prairie, a community of about six hundred located a few miles south of Hutchinson, Kansas. According to local lore, one of the first homesteaders a century ago exclaimed, "My, what a pretty prairie," and the town got its name. Of course, like most settlers on the plains, they immediately began to plant trees and to turn the prairie grass under but it is still an attractive area.

Besides its bucolic splendor Pretty Prairie is also famous for its mid-July rodeo. Now this is wheat country, an area settled by Mennonite farmers, and doesn't look like prime rodeo country, but for over fifty years Pretty Prairie has sponsored what the billboards leading into town proudly proclaim to be "Kansas' Largest Nite Rodeo." This rodeo, like many throughout the plains, was an outgrowth of neighbors' getting together to watch the local kids ride and rope, in this case on the Henry Graber farm north of town. Henry's sons, Harry and Merle, joined with Harry Kautzer and W. W. Graber (no relation), then coach at the local high school, to sponsor the first professional rodeo in 1936. Since then, with one exception, Pretty Prairie has had a rodeo each year.

Over the years Pretty Prairie has surprised many first-time visitors who can't believe that a town so small and so completely surrounded by plowed fields could possibly put on a successful rodeo. Hadley Barrett, who has announced Pretty Prairie for nearly twenty years (and who has twice been selected by rodeo cowboys as the best announcer in the business), told me: "When I first came here I wondered where in the world they would get enough people to fill the stands. Then about seven o'clock they started streaming in, 8 and 10 abreast down the street. The grandstands here hold over 8,000 people, and I've seen 'em overflowing nearly every year."

Barrett, who has announced all the big rodeos, including the National Finals, uses Pretty Prairie as an example of rodeo at the grass roots. "When interviewers ask me about my favorite rodeos," he said, "I always mention Pretty Prairie." After attending, I can see why. It was a smoothly run affair with good stock and excellent specialty acts. But the biggest crowd pleaser was stock contractor Fred Dorenkamp's tiny four-year-old granddaughter, Kara, running steers and calves out of the arena on a big bay gelding.

The last surviving founder of the Pretty Prairie rodeo, W. W. Graber, had invited my wife and me to the 1986 rodeo. He and his wife treated us to a family gathering (their three daughters, sons-in-law, and grandchildren always come home for Christmas and for the rodeo) and to some of the best brisket, roasting ears, garden-fresh salads, and homemade bread, cake, and ice cream I have ever eaten. Graber had also arranged several interviews with rodeo officials and old-time cowboys. One of them was Gene Boyer, a Pretty Prairie native who bulldogged professionally for many years (from Cheyenne to Chicago) and who jumped his last steer at his hometown rodeo in 1980—when he was sixty-four years old.

But I believe that the most interesting experiences in Pretty Prairie—maybe in all the central plains—belong to W. W. Graber. A hometown boy who went to Bethel College and became a successful teacher and coach (his 1936 Pretty Prairie basketball team won a state championship), he returned to farming in the late 1930s, raising wheat and feeding cattle. He was one of the men who met in Byrd Hardy's barn in Greensburg in 1949 to form the Kansas Wheat Growers Association, and he later served as president of the Kansas Wheat Commission, which he also helped bring into existence.

For several months in the mid-1960s he flew at treetop level over thousands and thousands of square miles of Africa, searching for a suitable location for wheat production, part of an ambitious project sponsored by the Garvey Corporation of Wichita. He selected Morocco, set up headquarters in Casablanca, flew equipment in, hired and trained local help, and within three years had planted fifteen thousand acres of dryland wheat that produced forty bushels an acre.

Graber's modest demeanor and soft voice belie the depth and variety of his experiences, just as its quiet, slow-moving exterior masks the energy and community spirit of his hometown. I am looking forward to many more years of the Pretty Prairie rodeo.—*JH*

60. *Fred Beeson*

ONE OF THE COUNTRY'S very best ropers back in the Roaring Twenties was Fred Beeson of Arkansas City, Kansas. He learned to rope as a youngster on his father's farm and perfected his skills while working for the world-renowned Miller Brothers' 101 Ranch near Ponca City, Oklahoma. At least that is what I have surmised from the scant surviving evidence. A few rodeo programs listing his name and some newspaper clippings, most of them undated, contain most of what I've been able to find out about him.

Beeson was born four miles east of Arkansas City on February 7, 1889, and started rodeoing in 1915. He must have had a lot of tenacity and a strong sense of self-worth, because most ropers would never have tried a second year if their first was as bad as his had been. According to the November 1915 issue of *The Wild Bunch,* Beeson had shipped his roping horse over five thousand miles that year and had won only ten dollars. Rodeo historian Willard Porter (who pointed this item out to me) considers Beeson one of the pioneers who helped to give rodeo a firm footing by continuing to compete despite the hard times, difficulty of travel, and low purses.

By the end of the teens, however, Beeson had established himself as the roper to beat. He had set a record (eight seconds) in the breakaway steer roping at Phoenix and he won the steer roping at the Pendleton Stampede in 1919. In 1916 he placed second in calf roping (and won sixteen hundred dollars) at a New York rodeo sponsored by Teddy Roosevelt. He established a world's record for calf roping (seventeen seconds) at a rodeo in Detroit, which doesn't sound very fast today, but his goat-roping record (nine seconds) does. He traveled with the 101 Ranch Wild West Show and at least twice performed in Europe.

His biggest triumphs came at the Cheyenne Frontier Days, the Daddy of 'em All. In the years before 1929, the year official championships began to be handed down by the Rodeo Association of America, the winner at Cheyenne was considered by his peers to be the world champion. Beeson won the first calf roping ever held at Cheyenne (in 1920) by averaging 45.3 seconds on three calves. Eight years later he won the steer roping, averaging 34.8 seconds on three head.

Beeson's practice arena was apparently the hangout of such early rodeo greats as Ben Johnson, Henry Grammer, Ike Rude, and Clay McGonigal. Will Rogers, also known to have some ability with a rope, once spent a day watching the action at the Beeson arena. He was playing a vaudeville date at the opera house in Arkansas City and apparently used his free time to pick up some pointers.

According to Ralph Reynolds, who was reared in Ark

City and knew the Beesons, Fred had a bronc-riding brother named Claude and a sister who lived in Maryland. Fred's father, Albert, operated a stud barn: two jacks, a Percheron, and a saddle horse. A lifelong bachelor, Fred retired from competition after being injured when his horse fell on him during the steer roping at Cheyenne (in either 1934 or 1944; records about his life, besides being sparse, are also inconsistent) and died at eighty-one in 1970.

Fred Beeson, it seems to me, deserves more commemoration than he has received.—*JH*

61. *Jay B. Parsons*

IN APRIL, 1986, I attended a meeting in Reno, Nevada, still the Biggest Little City in the World. But instead of spending all my spare time (and money) at the tables, I rented a car and drove over Donner Pass, site of the infamous cannibalism episode of 1846, to visit with a former plains dweller who now resides in the High Sierra.

Jay B. Parsons was born and reared in the Flint Hills near El Dorado, Kansas, more than seventy-five years, full years, ago. Although his was a farm family, Jay wanted to be a cowboy. There were plenty of role models to follow in northeast Butler County back in the 1920s, days when the Santa Fe stockyards at Chelsea, Aikman, and Cassoday funneled scores of thousands of Texas steers to and from their summer pastures of bluestem. Many of the working cowboys there were also good rodeo cowboys, and that bug bit Jay as well.

He still remembers his first rodeo: "I entered the calf roping at the Eureka rodeo just after I got out of high school. I borrowed Bus Young's horse, or maybe it was Frank's. Anway, I won second place and that ruined me. All I wanted to do after that was rodeo." Rodeo he did, joining the Cowboy's Turtle Association in the early 1940s,

shortly before entering the service in World War II. After
his discharge he roped calves and bulldogged even more
extensively, hitting some of the biggest rodeos in the West.
Jay is a cowboy of the Gary Cooper school—quiet, with
little inclination to boast about his own triumphs—but I
did manage to extract from him the fact that among his
wins was the calf-roping title at Prescott, Arizona, the rodeo
considered by many (other than people from Pecos, Texas)
to be the world's first. He was much more inclined to tell
about some of his foibles, such as learning to bulldog. His
parents were opposed to this dangerous sport, so Jay got a
friend, Chester Scribner, to haze for him and he jumped
his first steer in the family pasture. Unfortunately, the
steer suffered a broken neck and Jay was worried to death
about how he would break the news. Luckily for the two
boys a thunderstorm came up during the night and the
next morning a neighbor dropped in to say that one of the
Parsons animals seemed to have been hit by lightning.

In order not to worry his parents when he first entered
a real bulldogging contest, Jay went with Wilbur Countryman (area rancher and later a rodeo producer himself) to
a little show in Oklahoma. Unbeknownst to Jay, however,
his aunt was there and saw him perform. By the time he
got back home, his mother already had the bad news. The
die was cast.

After high school Jay got a job on a big ranch near
Magdalena, New Mexico. Then he worked on dude ranches
in Wyoming and Montana, where he met his wife, Polly, a
Kentucky girl. Perhaps it was her bluegrass influence, perhaps it was his love of horses and a challenge, but Jay soon
bought some race horses, and he has been in the racing
business ever since. After Montana the Parsons lived near
Benson, Arizona, for several years, then moved back to
Cody, Wyoming, and about a dozen years ago escaped the
northern winters by moving to Rough and Ready, California, "below the snow line and above the fog line."

"Lanty" reads the name on the license plate of his Mer-
cedes, "the name of the mare that bought the car and most

of this place," he told me. She and various of her offspring have won scores of races for Jay and Polly at tracks in Colorado, Wyoming, Arizona, California, and elsewhere. They also owned the grand champion halter horse, J B King, at the Denver stock show one year.

Despite all this success in the world of Big Time Rodeo, Big Time Horse Shows, and Big Time Horse Racing, and despite the fact that he now lives in northeast California, Jay Parsons is true to his plains roots. Along with his herd of brood mares he also keeps a few cows. On the day that I drove over to interview him, he and a few neighbors were getting ready to brand his calf crop, about two dozen crossbreds that showed plenty of evidence (both color and fight) of Brahma and longhorn. The help included Jay's son Butch and his wife (daughter of rodeo great Bill Linderman) from Wyoming; Jay's daughter Punkin, who helps train his race horses; his wife, Polly; and half a dozen others, including Frank Foster, an old-time Oregon bronc rider.

As I swung the gate for them and the younger cowboys got into the pen to wrestle the calves, Jay mounted a big bay gelding, shook out his nylon, and started snagging the heels of the calves. He looked right at home.—*JH*

62. *Range Round-Up*

IN THE SPRING of 1986 the Oklahoma Cattlemen's Association held its second annual Range Round-Up contest, where crews from a dozen working Oklahoma ranches compete against one another in six events closely related to actual ranch work. The setting, however, was a far cry from a hot, windy, sandy Oklahoma ranch. The events took place at night in air-conditioned comfort in the awesome (an overused word, but the only one that applies in this instance) Lazy E arena at Guthrie, Oklahoma. It's big enough to rope in crossways, much less down its considerable length.

What is especially interesting to me about this contest (and about similar ranch rodeos that are becoming more and more popular in Texas, Oklahoma, Kansas, and other plains states) is the similarity to early-day rodeos, back before professionalism set in, something it has now done with a vengeance. The Professional Rodeo Cowboys Association, for instance, doesn't have rodeos anymore, it has "prorodeos." The cowboys in the PRCA are plenty skilled, but many of them have learned their skills at a school put on by other professional rodeo cowboys; some of the top riders and ropers in the world would be pretty sorry help in gathering and working cattle.

The Range Round-Up, however, is amateur in the true sense of that oft-maligned term. The contestants are working cowboys (each must have been employed full time on the ranch for which he rides for at least six months prior to the competition) who are riding working cow horses (which must be owned either by the cowboy or by the ranch for which he works). Four of the six events are ones that were regularly scheduled in rodeos throughout the plains up until the later 1930s: calf branding, wild-cow milking, wild-horse racing, and saddle-bronc riding.

This last event is the only one that is part of a standard rodeo today—but in far different form. Range Round-Up contestants do ride out of a chute (it would be more fun to see them rope, blindfold, and saddle the bronc in the arena), but they ride with a stock saddle, not a contest bronc saddle, and there is no penalty for holding on with the free hand. In fact, of the six rides we saw (the competition is spread over two nights), only half made the whistle and only one rode with one hand.

Wild-horse racing and wild-cow milking are sometimes held at rodeos today (usually smaller ones in cattle country), but I don't think calf branding, where a roper snags a calf out of a herd of cows and calves and then drags it to a couple of holders who take off the rope and hold the calf down while a brander slaps a brand on it (with chalk dust rather than a hot iron), has been part of a regular rodeo for decades.

The other two events are cattle doctoring (team roping with a cowboy on the ground to slap chalk dust on the steer's head to signal time) and cattle penning. This last-named contest has been around for years, especially in California, where a regular association has been formed to standardize rules. At Guthrie a three-person team (cowgirls were working this and the calf-branding events) had to sort out three numbered cattle from a herd of a couple of dozen, then drive them into a small set of portable pens set up about a third of the way from the other end. Only four teams over the two-day contest got three head penned within the three-minute time limit.

A personal note: I took my father (Kenneth) and my uncle (Marshall) with me. The two of them represent more than a century and a half of cowboying, both the pasture and the rodeo varieties, and I figured that they could provide good running commentary. Sure enough, they had figured out a system to improve the effectiveness of cattle penning (send two men into the herd to cut out cattle) well before one of the teams did it (successfully) that way. And they thought that the bronc riding wasn't too impressive, but then these two had probably broken more horses, back in the years when nearly all unbroken horses bucked, than all the Range Round-Up contestants combined. We also enjoyed visiting with one of our old friends, Bobby Berger, a former world-champion bronc rider who was one of the three judges for the competition.

Some of the ranches represented included the famous Hitch Ranch (founded in 1884 when James Hitch bought some cattle at Dodge City and drove them into the then lawless no-man's-land of the Panhandle), the Stuart Ranch of Caddo (oldest family-owned ranch in Oklahoma, founded in 1868), and the Miller Ranch of Okmulgee (founded in the late 1870s). The winning ranch, however, was the newest, the Oklahoma Land and Cattle Company of Bartlesville, which has been operating 100,000 acres of Osage bluestem since 1953. This team didn't win a single contest, but, fittingly, it seems to me, for a contest designed to measure the all-around cattle-working ability of its hands and its horses, the crew from the Open A Bar placed in each event and had the highest point total.—*JH*

63. *The Fifty-Mile Horse Race*

A COUPLE OF YEARS back I read an article in some sports magazine about ride-and-tie races. I've forgotten all the details, but I do recall that there was a three-member team—two humans and a horse—and that one person would ride and the other run. After several miles the rider would dismount, tie the horse, and start running. The first runner would come upon the horse, mount and ride, go past the second runner, and then dismount and start running. The whole process was repeated over a course of many miles until all three members of the team had crossed the finish line.

At the time I read the article, I was reminded of the endurance races that were run early in this century, horse races that started in Omaha, for instance, and ended in Chicago five hundred miles away. Other races began at Chadron, Nebraska, adding some three hundred miles to the distance. Winning times, although measured in days, were surprisingly short.

Recently I learned of a horse race held in central Kansas for a couple of years after World War II, a race that started in Stafford and ended in Hutchinson, fifty miles away. I was visiting with an old friend, Floyd Rumford of Abbyville, and he showed me a photograph of himself, Bob Jones, and Gene Herrin, who finished one-two-three in the second year of the race.

Floyd also won the race the first year. He said that about a dozen men entered each year. Contestants left Stafford at five-minute intervals, having drawn for positions, and the winner was determined by elapsed time, not by order of finish. At Abbyville, exactly halfway between Hutchinson and Stafford, racers took a compulsory hour-long rest before beginning the final leg. Floyd said that old-timers who had run in some of the longer endurance races told him that the best way to win was to ride in a steady but hard jog the entire distance, that he would be passed at first but that the steady pace would eventually win out. He won the first race in a little over three hours (not counting the hour's rest in Abbyville), but not by following the advice of the veterans. Instead he ran his horse, then walked him when he needed a breather.

The horse Floyd was mounted on in the photograph was a wiry-looking little dun named Buckshot. He had bought him for sixty-five dollars at the Hutchinson horse auction, knowing nothing of his breeding except that he looked like a mustang. No matter how much feed he gave him, Floyd said, Buckshot never got fat. He just stayed lean and tough.

Bob Jones, a friend and fellow resident of Abbyville, was determined to beat Floyd the second year. He conditioned his horse by riding around a section—four miles— at a stiff gallop. Bob left Stafford in the third or fourth position, some fifteen or twenty minutes ahead of Floyd, who drew the seventh starting slot. They rode neck and neck into the Abbyville compulsory rest stop.

By the time he reached the finish line at Hutchinson, Floyd had passed everyone. He rode Buckshot at two speeds the entire distance—lope and run. His time: two hours and thirty-three minutes. They don't make many horses like that anymore!—*JH*

64. *Potato Races*

IN THE EARLIER YEARS of this century, before automotive power had displaced horsepower as a major mode of transport, plains dwellers loved to play games on horseback. Small plains towns on Saturday nights were filled with young men on horses (even after the Model T had become the family car), and county fairs and Fourth of July picnics had horse races of every imaginable kind—jockey, harness, relay, stake, horse versus man, etc. One popular type of horseback game was the potato race. Rules varied from place to place, but usually this contest involved transferring as many potatoes as possible from a basket at one end of the race course to a basket at the other. At Gove, Kansas, in the mid-1920s a potato race pitted one horseman against another in head-to-head competition (as television announcers like to say). Each contestant was armed with a sharpened lath and had to be mounted on a regular saddle horse, not a race horse or a pony or any other type of mount that might give one an unfair advantage. The contest, as I understand it, ran for a specified time (something like two minutes), with each contestant spearing potatoes at the starting point and dropping them off at the finish line. The winner was the one with the heavier basket.

At Cassoday, Kansas, in the first decade of this century potato races were a bit more rowdy. Contestants were mounted and armed with pointed laths, as at Gove, but instead of two individuals there were two teams and instead of a time limit the race ended when the first basket was filled. The complicating factor was that competitors were allowed to knock the potatoes off the sticks of their opponents. Swinging their laths like swords and crashing into one another, potato racers at Cassoday left the hundred-yard race course strewn with potatoes and an occasional horseman as spirits, and tempers, rose.

This contest, rowdy though it seems, strikes me as a rather tame analogue to the Afghan national sport, buzkashi. This event, which traces back to the Mongol hordes, is an every-man-for-himself, free-for-all, keep-away contest with as many as four hundred horsemen, each trying to gain possession of a headless, eviscerated calf or goat in order to carry it to a goal post on a race course over a mile long. For both men and horses, broken bones are commonplace and deaths are not rare.

Another type of potato race is analogous to the nine-teenth-century Mexican vaquero sport of rooster pulling—of burying chickens up to their necks, then racing by at top speed and reaching down from the saddle to jerk their heads off. Gory, but a real test of horsemanship. The potato race version, which took place in Texas in the early years of this century, had twenty potatoes lying on the ground spaced over a race course several hundred yards long. The contestant with the fastest time won, but in order to qualify the rider had to be traveling at least at a lope as he picked up each potato. A missed potato, or a slower gait, and he was disqualified.

The last record I have of a potato race is in the 1930s, but it's possible that some are still being held. I would enjoy seeing one.—*JH*

65. *Hawaiian Rodeo*

AT THE 1985 Western Social Sciences Association meeting Paul Bonnifield, a Great Plains historian (and railroad engineer) from Colorado who knows of my interest in rodeo history, passed along to me some photographs from his rodeoing experiences as a Navy man in Hawaii in the late 1950s. Except for the palm trees and surf in the background, most of the photographs could have been from rodeos anywhere on the plains.

Paul was driving a train (or whatever engineers do) and missed the 1986 meeting, but his wife, Ellen, brought me a copy of the program from the Navy Relief Fund Benefit Hawaiian Round-up, in which Paul had competed in 1959. The rodeo was held near Honolulu in an arena named for Fritz Truan, 1940 world-champion all-around cowboy. Truan, a Marine, had won the saddle-bronc contest at a Honolulu rodeo in early 1944, just months before losing his life in the assault on Iwo Jima.

Based on the fifteen events listed in the program, the

1959 rodeo seemed to me a mixture of modern and early-day rodeo as well as of horse show and shodeo. In addition to the seven standard events of a modern-day rodeo, there was also a relay race featuring three-member teams of riders. This rodeo event (only with one rider switching to three different horses) was very popular from the turn of the century until about World War II. There were junior divisions in calf roping, bull riding, and barrel racing (men and women competed equally in this last-named event), a reining contest for older men, and a jumping contest. The spear-and-ring race sounds like something from a Renaissance tournament.

There was also an event with an Hawaiian name, Poo Wai U, which may have been the Wild Ribbon Roping contest described elsewhere in the program but not otherwise named in the list of events. In mainland ribbon roping, generally speaking, a cowboy ropes a calf and a cowgirl strips a ribbon from its tail and runs to the finish line while the cowboy removes the rope from the calf. The Hawaiian version differed in having two cowboys, one to rope a yearling, another to strip the ribbon, then both removing the rope and running hand in hand back to the finish line.

I haven't learned how Paul fared at this rodeo (although one photograph shows him making a nice ride on a bareback bronc), but he was entered in five events: bareback (twenty riders), calf roping (twenty ropers), team roping (twenty-eight entries), senior barrel race (fifteen racers, of whom only two were cowgirls), and the relay race (nine teams). All told, an even one hundred people entered, sixty-two of them listing Hawaiian hometowns. About half of these names looked mainland to me, about half native. Of the thirty-eight other entries, three gave only a service (e.g., "Navy") as an address; six were from Texas; three each from South Dakota, Arizona, and Montana; two each from California, Wyoming, Oklahoma, and Louisiana; and one each from Canada, Mexico, Arkansas, Florida, Minnesota, Colorado, Nebraska, North Carolina, New Jersey, New York, Illinois, and Kentucky. Specialty acts included trick roper and whip artist Jack Wolfe, Patsy Trevene and her jumping horse Tejon, and rodeo clown and bullfighter Dick Tuell.

Despite my interest in the rodeo material, however, I have to admit that the most attention-getting item of information in the entire program was the twenty-two-cent hamburger advertised by Andy's Drive Inn.—*JH*

66. *Hawaiian Ropers*

IN THE LAST CHAPTER I described the 1959 Hawaiian Round-up, which traces back directly to the interest in rodeo generated by military personnel based in Hawaii during World War II. The majority of the contestants at these rodeos in the 1940s, '50s, and '60s, however, were Hawaiians. Some were originally from the mainland, but many were "paniolos"—native Hawaiian cowboys.

Few people know that one of the largest ranches in the United States is the Parker Ranch in Hawaii or that cattle were being raised on the Islands well before our West was even settled. I didn't know much about Hawaiian cowboys either until I had a chance to review a book manuscript, *The Aloha Cowboy*, by Virginia Cowan-Smith and Bonnie Domrose Stone.

Rodeo itself was developed on the Great Plains around mid–nineteenth century, although the paniolo, like the Spanish vaquero, had been riding and roping much earlier. Thus when he got a chance to participate in some of the early rodeos, the Hawaiian cowboy surprised his mainland counterparts, especially in roping. The earliest documented rodeolike contests in Hawaii occurred in 1903, only six years after Cheyenne began its Frontier Days, the Daddy of 'em All.

In a 1905 Wild West Show in Honolulu, Ikua Purdy set a record by tying a steer in less than forty seconds. Two years later a champion Wyoming roper in Buffalo Bill's

Wild West, Angus MacPhee, competed against—and lost to—Hawaiian ropers in three contests. The success of the Hawaiian locals gave "Rawhide Ben" Low the idea of sending a delegation of Hawaiian ropers to the Cheyenne rodeo the next year. The gamble paid off even better than he had hoped. Ikua Purdy, considered by many to be Hawaii's best roper ever, won the Cheyenne steer roping in 1908 with a time of fifty-six seconds. Archie Kaaua took third place and Jack Low sixth. Commentators noted not only the outstanding roping skills of the Islanders but also the excellent horses upon which they were mounted. (Any roper will tell you that his horse is worth a good 75 percent of any success he has.)

Rodeos and Wild West shows grew in popularity during the teens and twenties in the Islands, although most Hawaiians were ropers, not bronc riders (James Tripp being a notable exception). One reason for the skill of the paniolo ropers may have been that they were often operating in heavy tropical vegetation. They had to rope quickly and unerringly if they were to succeed in range work, and these traits carried over into their competitions.

Another legendary Hawaiian roper was Sebastian Reiny, whose background is uncertain but who was a veteran of the U.S. Cavalry and who was reputed to have been highly successful on the mainland rodeo circuit in the 1930s. Reiny is said to have been able to rope anything that moved and to do it so fast that the eye could hardly follow his movements. More than one story is told of his roping a running bull while mounted backwards on his horse.

Interest in rodeo in Hawaii declined in the thirties. Ikua Purdy, a quiet man, never returned to Cheyenne to defend his title. He returned to ranch work in 1920, where he was said never to have missed when he threw a rope. He died on July 4, 1945—just about the time that many mainland soldiers and sailors thought they were introducing rodeo to the Islands.—*JH*

67. *Canadian Football*

I'M NOT THE FIRST or the only writer who has observed how important football is to the culture of towns on the American plains, especially, I think, the southern plains. So in the course of a summer's study of the Canadian plains in Saskatchewan, I made it a point to take in a night game of the Canadian Football League. The contest I witnessed on June 14, 1985, was an exhibition match between the Edmonton Eskimos and the Saskatchewan Roughriders in Regina. (The home team won on a field goal.)

Sports eccentrics who follow the Canadian game know that there are distinct differences between the Canadian and American brands of football. The Canadian playing field, for instance, is 110 yards long and also correspondingly wider than its American counterpart. The end zones are deeper, too. I attended the Roughriders game with Bruce Shepard, a civil servant from Regina, and I told him that the field was so big the owners ought to replace the artificial turf with bromegrass and lease the place for pasture between games.

Other obvious differences: twelve men on a side instead of eleven; three downs instead of four to make ten yards; and no rules regulating offensive men in motion. A Canadian backfield mills around before each play like a bunch of scaled quail contemplating flight and then suddenly bursts into the defensive secondary. From these variances in rules derive differences in style: the Canadian game seems to be composed of about two-thirds passing and one-third kicking.

Kicking is especially important because of what are called "singles"—not "extra points" but single points scored by punting or place-kicking the ball so deep into the opponent's endzone that he does not run it out. Singles are one feature of the game that show it to be slightly closer akin to English rugby than is American football.

This observation about rugby leads to a generalization about the sports life of the northern plains: that despite the array of ethnic settlers who populated the region, the traditions of the British Isles were dominant. It may not be complimentary to British culture to note, of course, that its two most successful sporting transplants to the Canadian plains were rather barbaric games: curling (a contest in which competitors hurl granite stones across ice) and rugby (self-evidently a form of organized mayhem).

Inevitably, though, American immigrants, the same folks who brought to the Canadian plains such wonders as mechanized agriculture and the Ku Klux Klan, bent British sports traditions into American patterns. The Saskatchewan Roughriders were founded in 1910 as a rugby club, but, like other such clubs, played a game that became year by year more like American football. In fact the team started out with a name—the Roughriders—obviously derived from the military exploits of former Dakota rancher Teddy Roosevelt.

In recent years media influence has compounded the Americanization, including the addition of scantily clad cheerleaders to keep the television cameras busy between plays. If any bit of indigenous Saskatchewaniana remains, it must be the team mascot, Gainer the Gopher, although I'm still not sure why a historic agricultural pest deserves such enshrinement.

The point is that Canadian football now resembles American football much more than it does the common antecedent of both sports, English rugby. And ties between the two North American games continue. Canadian prep stars go south to get athletic scholarships, and American college standouts go north to get pro contracts, although each Canadian club is limited to fifteen "imports" (American players).

Here is a final fragment of football lore I offer for Sooner fans in Oklahoma. Do you know where Washington State got its Heisman Trophy candidate, Reuben Mayes? He came south from North Battleford, Saskatchewan. And the reason his family lived in North Battleford, Bruce Shepard says, was that at the time Oklahoma became a state, hundreds of black farmers, unwilling to be governed by the white Democrats who were sure to control the Oklahoma statehouse, emigrated to Saskatchewan.—*TI*

Part Five

A HARD LIFE IN A HARD COUNTRY

T.A. SON

PHOTOGRAPHIC
STUDIO

68.   *A Hard Country*

YOU CAN LEARN things by studying old photographs, things that the figures in them perhaps didn't intend to convey. For instance, I'm looking at a photograph now. It's a picture of my Great-Grandfather Adolph Isern, his wife, Wilhelmine, and their three boys, Alvin, Alfred, and Walter. It was taken during the 1890s, about twenty years after Adolph and Wilhelmine had settled on a quarter of land in Barton County, Kansas, purchased for them by Great-Great-Grandfather Fritz Isern from the Santa Fe Railroad.

Uncle Alvin in this photograph is wearing an old suit much too small for him and holding the bridle of a plow horse. Uncle Walter is wearing a new suit that fits perfectly and carrying a croquet mallet. It should come as no surprise to learn that Uncle Alvin stayed on the farm, while Uncle Walter joined a mercantile firm.

Now I look at the two central figures, Adolph and Wilhelmine. Adolph is a slight, bearded gentleman, a sensitive-looking fellow. Wilhelmine is a big, sturdy, grim woman. Adolph and Wilhelmine, natives of the north German province of Hanover, came to Kansas from Ohio.

The frame house, windmill, and croquet set in the photo attest to a degree of prosperity—but Adolph and Wilhelmine don't look very happy. By this time they have put in two decades of hard work, hard enough to break down a sensitive man and to harden a tough woman. Looking at their modest success, I wonder if they think it was worth the effort.

What Adolph and Wilhelmine had in common with all the other immigrants to the plains, whether they were Prussians in Texas or Ukranians in Saskatchewan, was that they came to a hard country. A country short on timber, rainfall, capital, and society. They either failed on the plains or they learned to adapt to them, and in adaptation they had to cast aside many of their beloved ways and customs. That process of abandonment is the thought behind this little essay.

The Iserns in Ohio had become accustomed to raising and preserving their own fruit. So, as I know from reading the manuscript census, by 1885 Adolph and Wilhelmine had set out four hundred peach trees and lesser numbers of plum, cherry, and apple. I look at Great-Grandma Wilhelmine's shoulders, and they are broad, but not enough so to carry water to all those peach trees. They died before the 1895 state census. I can't recall any fruit trees at all on the various Isern farms where I grew up, but I remember that my grandparents always referred to the groves of elm, locust, and maple around the places as "the orchard."

One grove stands in a half-acre of ground with the remnants of a low dike still discernible around it. Recently I have pondered why people would refer to the mass of trees that stood in that diked area as "the pond."

The Iserns were a bunch of north Germans, and as such they were accustomed to fish in their diet—a preference sustainable in Ohio, but not in Kansas. The move west must have presented a dietary crisis.

The logical response was for Great-Grandma Wilhelmine to put the men to work building a carp pond. Exactly why the pond didn't pan out, I don't know; I suspect the pond failed to seal. I do know that by the time of my generation, nobody ate much fish. My cousin Bernice says that Great-Great-Grandfather Fritz sent a barrel of herring to his children in Kansas every winter. It was the least he could do after sticking them out there on those Santa Fe quarter sections!

These examples of fruit culture and fish eating have something to say about what Jim and I have been trying to do the past few years in our *Plains Folk* writings. We maintain that there is such a thing as a culture of the Great Plains, a set of attitudes and ways distinctive of the broad region stretching from Texas to Saskatchewan. What we have to admit at the outset is that this regional culture began with the destruction of many of the cultural attributes brought to the area by immigrants.

That's why I wish that the photographer who shot this picture had included a few of Wilhelmine's peach trees, even if he had had to leave out Walter's croquet mallet.—*TI*

69. *Bindweed Mythology*

I HAVE COMMENTED in past writings about the persistence of mythology in the modern culture of the Great Plains. Myths are the stories that we tell to show how things came to be the way they are. They may be true or they may be bunk, but that isn't the point. When people develop a myth about something, that means they consider it important or intriguing.

Jim has written about the common practice of burning pastures to promote growth of grass and to control weeds and brush. You can tell that pasture burning is important where it is practiced, because people have a myth about it. They say that Indians began the custom of burning the grasslands in order to attract game. I don't disagree with the practice of pasture burning and the Indian story may be true, but there's no sound evidence that it is.

People throughout the plains perpetuate myths about their climate, especially the story that weather runs according to seven-year cycles. Seven wet years, seven dry years, and so on. It's quite biblical. My friend Charley Webb, a geographer, says that there's nothing to this, however. He has put the rainfall data through every pattern that he can think of, and there just aren't any such short-term cycles.

Mythology is particularly prevalent in regard to the origins of agricultural pests, both animal and plant. Agricultural scientists seem just as prone to cite these myths as are other folk. In their bulletins, for instance, they repeat the old story that Hessian flies came to North America with Hessian mercenary troops fighting against the American Revolution. There is a myth about potato bugs, too. Potato bugs are native to the Rocky Mountains, where, before the arrival of domestic potatoes, they fed only on a particular weed. The story is that they crossed the plains east with freight wagons plying the route between the Colorado goldfields and the Missouri River, thereby meeting the advancing agricultural frontier.

A sinister myth of origin says that German-Russian immigrants brought the seed of Russian thistles to the plains to sow in the fields of their enemies (whoever their enemies were, which is never clear). Another myth asserts that sunflowers are not indigenous to Kansas, the state that has designated them its state flower. Ostensibly sunflowers traveled to Kansas from New Mexico in the running gear of wagons along the Santa Fe Trail.

All this is preface to my comments about the common myth as to the origins of field bindweed on the plains. Here again the Germans from Russia, both Mennonite and Volga Deutsch, are supposed to take the blame. This story generally concedes how nice it was that these folks brought hard red winter wheat to the plains, but mourns that mixed in with the wheat was the seed of bindweed.

The story is the more confusing because there are two main types of bindweed in North America: field bindweed, which is a major noxious weed of the plains and originated in Europe and Asia, and hedge bindweed, which is less of a pest and is native to North America.

It is likely that field bindweed did travel to the North American plains with German-Russian immigrants. It is also likely, though, that it came to the Atlantic coast much earlier, during colonial times, traveled westward with the farming frontier, and then exploded into a major pest when the frontier reached the weed's most favorable environment, the plains.—*TI*

70. *Hardy Bindweed*

MYTHS ABOUT the origins of animals and plants, such as those about bindweed, show that ordinary people recognize, as do plant breeders, that living things introduced from a distant point of origin often show remarkable vigor in their new home. Even King David wrote in Psalm 80, speaking of the people of Israel, "Thou didst bring a vine out of Egypt; and it took root and filled the land."

That's just what field bindweed did in the central and southern plains. Field bindweed is such a serious pest on the plains because it is so hardy. It competes best against domestic plants where the climate is subhumid to semiarid.

Bindweed eventually spread all over the region through a variety of means of transport—in threshing machines, in seed, with birds and animals. Once established, agricultural scientists calculated, it doubled its coverage every five years.

Bindweed, sometimes called wild morning glory, is a rather attractive plant with deep-green leaves and pinkish-white blossoms. It's the part of the plant underground that's treacherous. Its roots extend both laterally and deep, to several feet below the surface. Plants may spring from buds at any point along these roots. The persistent roots make the plant difficult to eradicate. They also assist it in efficient gathering of moisture from the soil, which is why bindweed is so damaging to crops.

The main weapon in the battle against bindweed today is 2,4-D. Agricultural scientists may talk of using competitive crops and appropriate tillage to assist in control of the weed, but farmers largely place their faith in the herbicide.

This does raise one problem peculiar to the plains. Herbicides work best on weeds that are growing vigorously in the presence of adequate moisture. The infrequency of rainfall on the plains means that there are long times within a year when herbicides are relatively ineffective. Still, few farms would like to go back to the era prior to the advent of 2,4-D. The experiences of those times make an interesting study in how the folk methods of farming strived to cope with a problem for which science provided no adequate answer.

The initial method most farmers used against bindweed was persistent tillage. During the early years of the twentieth century, however, they generally found existing implements inadequate for bindweed, and so they built or adapted their own on the farm. A common adaptation was to convert an old drill frame or cultivator frame into what was called a "duckfoot" by mounting V-shaped sweeps on it.

Some still feared that bindweed would slip between the sweeps unscathed. Such meticulous fellows might mount a single, long straight blade on the frame from an old lister. The blade was usually salvaged from a grader or a stalk cutter.

All these special adaptations for bindweed eradication seemed peculiar at the time. To anyone familiar with modern implements for conservation tillage, though, they would look rather familiar, at least in principle. These innovative tillage implements were just the beginning of farmers' tactics against bindweed.—*TI*

71. *The Battle against Bindweed*

AFTER FARMERS FOUND tillage a tiresome method of staying on top of bindweed infestations, but still before the advent of 2,4-D, they tried other tactics. Smothering was one of these. This method was appropriate only against small patches of the weed, because it required piling straw—or sometimes unrolling rolls of tar paper—on top of the weed. Not only was this a lot of work, but the bindweed also tended to come back as sassy as ever after the period of smothering.

In order to avoid taking land out of production for the smothering process, and also because it generally was more effective, people commonly used a growing crop as the smothering agent. Alfalfa was good for this. A thick stand of alfalfa, regularly cut, competed quite well against bindweed. If it didn't destroy the weed, it at least greatly reduced it.

Chemical methods of control before 2,4-D were crude and not too effective. Kerosene, or more commonly salt in rock or brine form, appeared to hit the surface foliage pretty hard, but the roots survived almost unaffected. However, the last time I talked to old Ezra Blackmon, who at that time owned and produced commercial salt at the Big Salt Plain of northwestern Oklahoma, he still insisted that brine from his salt wells was the best remedy for bindweed. He said you had to spread it evenly over the surface of the ground and make a crust in order to prevent the bindweed from recurring.

Sodium chlorate, commonly used during the 1920s and 1930s, marked the next stage in chemical development against bindweed. This stuff, although effective if followed up with tillage, was so expensive and hazardous that few used it on any but small acreages.

Finally, there were animal controls that could be used against bindweed. Folks with sheep fenced off patches of bindweed and let the sheep crop the surface foliage off closely.

But sheep were not nearly as effective as were hogs. At this time people generally put their sows and pigs on hog pasture anyway. When they fenced off patches of bindweed as pasture, the hogs not only ate the foliage but also grubbed out the roots assiduously, providing they had been turned out with their snouts unringed. The only problem with this method was that it left the patch looking like a mine field afterward.

Albert Stolfus from here in Lyon County, Kansas, told me about using hogs to clear out three acres of bindweed on his place. "I just turned the hogs in there, and when they got through with that, it was so rough you could hardly drive a team of horses over it with a disk or harrow," he said. "Holes so big all over that three acres. But they fixed it. They cleaned it out."

Most states ultimately designated bindweed a noxious weed, established control districts, and sent out inspectors to deal with it. Organized efforts to combat the weed generally emphasized the same sort of folk methods that I have talked about. Not until the advent of 2,4-D after World War II was there any more effective means.

During World War II, when bindweed was a rampant problem and people lacked means to control it, bureaucrats involved in noxious-weed programs loved to talk in military terms about the "battle of the bindweed." So I guess it was appropriate that the ultimate solution to the problem, 2,4-D, was a chemical with close ties to the military for use as a defoliant.—TI

72. *Broomweeds*

LIVING IN THE Flint Hills region, I have become familiar with the plant known around here as broomweed, or, among some old-timers, as snakeweed. It was only during the past few years, however, that I learned that this weed is distinct from another yellow-flowered pasture weed of the same genus commonly called broom snakeweed. The broomweed differs from the broom snakeweed in that the broomweed has a single, fairly heavy stem coming up ten to twelve inches from the ground, where it branches into the multiple stems from which the name of the plant derives; the broom snakeweed has multiple stems from the ground up. Moreover, whereas the broomweed, an annual, is a weed of the southeastern plains, the broom snakeweed, a perennial, is a weed of the southwestern plains. (States from Nebraska north are largely free of either weed.)

People in the rangelands of the southeastern plains seem to worry a lot about broomweeds. Stands of broomweeds in pastures get particularly heavy during wet years that follow years of drought. For instance, after the severe drought year of 1936, broomweeds blanketed the hillsides in 1937. In those times, because the annual weeds reproduced from seed, range-management specialists advised pasture owners to mow the weeds before they could go to seed in the fall.

The idea was that the broomweeds were a threat to usurp land from productive grass. Nowadays, thought about this has changed, relates Clenton Owensby, a nationally known scholar of range management from Kansas State University. Owensby says that during the summer of 1981, a wet year that followed a dry year, he had a "jillion" calls from people asking what to do about the infestation of broomweeds. His advice was, "Do nothing." "If you don't like it," he said, "just wait until next year, and it will go away." His point was that the broomweed is an emphemeral weed, that is, one that comes and goes with temporary conditions. Broomweeds don't take ground over from grass; they just fill ground where the grass has died out, and in that sense, they may serve a good purpose in preventing erosion of bare ground.

Broomweeds, then, are nothing to worry about. In fact, many folks in this part of the country put the dried weeds to ornamental use in arrangements. My wife has a basket of them in our parlor at home. I often see bunches of them for sale in craft stores, which goes to show how easily some people can be fooled. Some ladies in the southern Flint Hills even have told me broomweeds make a medicinal tea (Owensby advises against such use).

Perennial broom snakeweed, on the other hand, is another matter, for this more aggressive weed can usurp ground from grass. Owensby says that the reason why broom snakeweed is becoming a problem on the southern plains of New Mexico and West Texas, a situation that I have been reading about in farm periodicals, is that the two things that historically kept the weed in check—fire and wild grazing animals—are now absent from the scene. Pasture owners on the southwestern plains do not commonly burn their pastures, as many on the southeastern plains do. Neither are there enough antelope, prairie dogs, or other such indiscriminate grazers to keep the plants in check.

Consequently, weed-control specialists on the southwestern plains have been urging pasture owners to attack infestations of broom snakeweed with herbicides in the fall, when the plants are growing vigorously. I have another idea as to how to get rid of this herbal pest. The folks in the southwestern plains ought to take a cue from the craft-shop owners around here, or perhaps a better model would be the promoters who convinced people that ginseng, a forest plant, was an aphrodisiac, thereby ensuring that foragers would practically wipe out that species in North America. Why not just put out the word in New Jersey and California that this rare ornamental, the broom snakeweed, is fetching fancy prices? Urban folk no doubt will descend upon the countryside, taking up the slack left by the absence of natural grazers.—*TI*

73. *Rock Pickers and Swathers*

IF YOU'RE GOING to be in Saskatchewan in June, everyone said, don't miss the Western Canada Farm Progress Show. Convened annually in Regina and billed as the world's largest exhibition of dryland farming technology, the WCFP Show is to the Canadian plains what the 3I Show (held by alternate years in Great Bend and Garden City, Kansas) is to the southern plains.

I regarded the WCFP Show as a good opportunity to compare and contrast the agricultural ways of the north with those of the south, and I was not disappointed. The similarities were the things that seem commonplace to plains folk: economies of scale, emphasis on wheat, innovations in tillage, and fascination with combines. It was the differences that particularly intrigued me.

For instance, there were quite a few exhibitors who either would not or could not have come to an American show. The Australians, old comrades of the Canadians in the British Commonwealth, were there in force, engaging in a sort of negative geographic one-upsmanship. Their implement men made an argument along these lines: you may think you have a tough, arid land to farm here in

North America, but compared to Australia, it's a rose garden; we have devised equipment sturdy enough for our harsh conditions at home, so just think how well it will work here.

Then there were the representatives of the Communist European nations. I noticed, however, that the exhibits of the Russian and Romanian firms were little attended. It happened that I was touring them with a veteran administrator of the Saskatchewan Agricultural Implements Board, which regulates equipment sales in the province, and he was noticeably unimpressed.

To me as a southern plainsman, the most intriguing oddities were the ingenious devices to remove rocks from fields. To people who live in territories never touched by glaciers, this may seem like a trivial enterprise, but in that land of glacial till, there are folks farming their grandparents' homesteads who still bring up reefs of pesky granite rocks every time they stir the soil.

In response to this problem, a half-dozen firms offer sturdy rock rakes that swath the stones into windrows like hay. Stones in such windrows may be gathered together with rock pickers—heavy, tractor-drawn carts with pick-up fingers on a reel in front. Entrepreneurs with elaborate rock-picking machinery often do custom work.

Mention of entrepreneurs reminds me of two truly notable characters who had exhibits in the hall reserved for new inventions. The first of them was Jake Dietz of Craik, Saskatchewan. He makes giant grain swathers—the largest cuts a seventy-five-foot swath—that swing behind a tractor to go down the road. He says you can tell a wheat farmer's politics by how he harvests. Jake is CCF (Cooperative Commonwealth Federation), and he doesn't think much of the Conservatives (the current ruling party in Canada). Good CCFers, he contends, all harvest with swathers. Only bullheaded Conservatives think they can straight-combine spring wheat.

When he made this remark, Dietz nodded toward the other exhibitor, a neighbor of his in Craik, Bert Wilfong.

Wilfong is a longtime custom combiner in both Canada and the United States. He also is a big-time dryland farmer in Colorado; in fact, promoters of sodbuster legislation point to him as a prime example of a foreign operator breaking unstable grassland regardless of the consequences. At the show he was promoting customized cylinders for combines—straight-cutting combines, I guess—Dietz says he's a Conservative.—*TI*

74. Cutting Wood

LIKE HUNTING or fishing, cutting firewood is a primordial pursuit. There seems to be something innately satisfying about burning the firewood you yourself have cut—at least if the number of people who take to the creeks and woodlots every fall with chain saws and power splitters is any indication. The appeal, I believe, goes beyond nostalgia for our pioneer past; woodcutting is Promethean, mythically linked with our first emergence from savagery into civilization. Thus the energy crisis of a decade ago not only brought about a boom in the sales of fireplace inserts, it also brought a horde of repressed woodsmen out of the closet.

I got to musing about all this a few weeks ago when my sister and her husband joined my son and me at Cassoday to saw up a bunch of wood that Dad had had piled up, some of it for a couple of years or more. Much of it was white or red elm (from trimming he had done in the windbreak) and there was quite a bit of hedge (or Osage orange or bois d'arc; the name varies with regional usage), including many old fence posts. If there is a hotter firewood than hedge posts a quarter- to a half-century old, I don't know what it would be! There were a few logs of apple and cedar and black locust, all of it good wood except for some of the older white elm that had become punky.

We sawed the wood with a tractor and buzz saw, just the way I remembered doing it when I was growing up and we heated exclusively with wood. We always had a huge wood-pile then, and every night after school my sister and I had the job of keeping the woodbox full. A few armloads of smaller sticks, along with a big chunk for overnight, would usually replenish the wood that had been burned during the day. I don't remember the brand name on our stove, but I do remember that it was made in Gadsden, Alabama.

I think I was in my teens when Dad got his first chain saw, a big yellow monster that I can hardly lift even today. Despite its weight and awkwardness, however, it was less tiring than a crosscut saw.

I still remember the first tree I ever cut down, an elm maybe four inches thick. My father and grandfather were cutting wood in the forty west of the house and I had gone out with them, armed with a little short-handled hatchet. I cut the tree shoulder high (about three feet off the ground), chopping all around it until it finally fell. I felt pretty cocky until Dadhoy said something humorous about beavers. He liked his trees cut smooth and close to the ground.

In the days before tractors one man in the area would often have a stationary engine and a buzz saw, cutting wood for shares or for cash. My father and uncle have told me that when they were in school, Christmas vacation was not something to look forward to—that's when they made wood for the following year. For days on end they would help cut trees, dragging them from the creek to the yard with mules, then neighbors would come in to help with the sawing, a pile of green wood growing bigger and bigger beside the pile of cured wood that was being used that winter.

I believe that if we modern-day Paul Bunyans had to rely on axes and crosscut saws and wedges, rather than on power equipment, most of us would soon revert to buying wood by the cord, stacked in the garage, if not entirely to fuel oil or propane.—*JH*

75. *The Dust Bowl*

IN FEBRUARY 1985 the Center for Great Plains Studies here at Emporia State University held a seminar on the Dust Bowl, my part of which was to talk about the literary response to this phenomenon. Tom handled the social effects while others talked about the geological and climatic causes and the political effects.

I was born at the tail end of the Great Depression of the Dirty Thirties (and well to the east of the worst dust), so, although I've heard many stories about both, I have no firsthand recollections of either. I do remember vividly the Filthy Fifties, when we certainly had plenty of dust in the air and no rain to clear it. I would be sent out on the tractor to disk alternating strips of a forty-acre field that was blowing so bad that you couldn't begin to see the other side. I can imagine what the section-size tracts out on the High Plains must have been like.

At least I think I can, but reading what people who lived through it have written and hearing the stories of the survivors makes me realize that the dust storms I drove through in western Kansas in the early 1960s, where the dirt was drifted like snow along the side of the road and headlights at two in the afternoon didn't illuminate more than a few dozen yards in front of the car, were nothing compared to the rollers that swept in like black blizzards back in the thirties.

"Roller" was the term used for the worst of the storms, the huge, towering, billowing clouds of dust that covered enormous areas. Weather personnel at Amarillo classified dusters into two types, the southwestern and the northern. The first filled the air with dust, but it was the second type that brought in the black blizzards. The Kansas Academy of Science recognized seven classes of dust storms, ranging from relatively minor "sand blows" to the awe-inspiring "funnel storms" that would lift dust into the air as high as four miles and carry it as far away as two or three thousand miles.

The most famous roller of all struck "on the fourteenth day of April, in nineteen-thirty-five," in the words of one of Woody Guthrie's Dust Bowl ballads. Guthrie was in Pampa, Texas, at the time, and he, like many others, had some definite intimations of mortality when that Sunday afternoon suddenly turned into night. Earlier, the storm had put a sudden end to a big rabbit drive (a favorite Dust Bowl pastime because jackrabbits were about the only thing that thrived during these desolate times) at Hooker, Oklahoma. Still earlier, as Dodge City was being engulfed, a postcard photographer had recorded the scene. In fact, a large number of the best Dust Bowl photographs are from the studio of this Dodge City entrepreneur.

Another thing that makes this particular storm so memorable is that it is the one that gave the era its name. A story describing the roller, filed by AP stringer Robert Geiger out of Guymon, Oklahoma, contained this line: "Three little words—achingly familiar on a western farmer's tongue—rule life today in the dust bowl of the continent . . . 'if it rains.'" The papers back east picked up the phrase and soon it was, and will remain forever, a part of the vocabulary of the Great Plains and of the nation.—*JH*

76. *Dust Bowl Literature*

OUR SEMINAR on the Dust Bowl, mentioned in the last chapter, was, in the jargon of my profession, a real learning experience, at least for me. We opened with a showing of the 1936 documentary *The Plow that Broke the Plains*, a title with at least three levels of meaning. Actually, the film is more propaganda than documentary, for its purpose was to show that the plowing up of the High Plains (in a frenzy of wheat-growing activity during and after World

War I) not only broke the sod but also broke the plains, both economically and spiritually. Pare Lorentz, the director, produced a work of genuine cinematic art, even if it was a little heavy handed on assessing blame (capitalistic exploiters) and labeling heroes (FDR's New Deal programs). The truth, it seems to me, was somewhere in between. I would be interested in learning of the reaction of Dust Bowl dwellers to the film when it was released. Seen now, fifty years later, it certainly makes a powerful statement.

So does the film with which we closed the seminar: John Steinbeck's *The Grapes of Wrath.* I don't know whether this was the first movie I ever saw, but it's the first one I remember seeing—projected on a sheet hanging from the wall of the high school gym. This was sometime during the later 1940s, a time when movies were often shown this way (or on a sheet hung outdoors on the side of some building) in small towns.

The movie, released in 1940, is more optimistic and less sensational (for its time) than was the novel, published a year earlier. The book was an immediate best seller, doing for Okies in California what *Uncle Tom's Cabin* had earlier done for slaves in the Old South. But despite the literary quality of the book (Steinbeck deserved his Nobel Prize), it has almost nothing to do with the Dust Bowl. The Joads are sharecroppers from the cotton country of eastern Oklahoma, and they are driven out by tractors and big landowners, not by dust storms.

One thing I discovered in preparing for this seminar is that there is precious little Dust Bowl literature. The one true Dust Bowl novel of any literary reputation is Frederick Manfred's *The Golden Bowl,* set in south-central South Dakota in the mid-1930s. Here a young drifter from Oklahoma is taken in by a farm family that has lost a son to a dust storm. One detail in the novel—a fissure in the earth big enough for a man or a horse to fall into, literally out of sight—seems a bit unrealistic to me, but maybe I just don't know the nature of the soil a couple of dozen miles east of the Badlands. Other than that the scenes of coping with the dust and the economic deprivation are depressingly realistic.

The best poetry from the era is found in the lyrics of Woody Guthrie's Dust Bowl ballads, even though some of these songs, like Steinbeck's novel, really deal more with the plight of the Okie in California than they do with the farmer on the High Plains. A song like "Dust Bowl Disaster," based on the infamous storm of April 14, 1935, conveys the sense of awe and fear that many Dust Bowl residents experienced when confronted with the immensity of these natural phenomena.—*JH*

77. *Dust Bowl Stories*

HISTORIES OF the Dust Bowl (such as those of Doug Hurt or Paul Bonnifield) give one a good idea of life during those dark times. Personal memoirs like Anne Marie Low's *Dust Bowl Diary* or W. J. Morton's *Snowstorms, Dust Storms and Horses' Tails* give an even more vivid account. Hearing the stories told firsthand by people who were actually there, however, is the best way to gain some sort of idea of what life then was really like.

The most popular part of our seminar on the Dust Bowl was a panel of Emporia State University faculty members who were there when it happened. Here are some of their stories. Tom Bridge was a farm boy in Baca County, Colorado; Gene Crawford was the son of a Dodge City railroad engineer; and Galen Neufeldt, born too late for the Dust Bowl proper but in plenty of time for the Filthy Fifties, was reared on a farm in Beaver County, Oklahoma. John Ransom, who couldn't attend the seminar but sent in a story or two with some of the others, lived on a farm in the northern Texas Panhandle. Connect all these points on a map and you have the outline of the very heart of the Dust Bowl.

Some recalled Woody Guthrie's Black Sunday of April 14,

1935. Crawford remembers playing outside on Black Sunday when his grandmother started yelling and pointing. He turned to the north and saw what looked like a giant rolling pin—a two- or three-thousand-foot-high rolling cloud of black dust. His mother got through the storm to their house by wrapping a wet towel completely around her head (she couldn't see anything anyway) and walking with one foot on the sidewalk and one on the ground until she hit—physically—the cinder-block fence around their yard. After this storm they sealed their house as best they could with tape. Following another duster, Mrs. Crawford swept up the dirt that had drifted around only one taped window and carried it to the grocery store scales to be weighed—twelves pounds of dust! She remembers that the dust seemed almost to come in through the glass.

Black Sunday, to Tom Bridge, doesn't stand out among the many dust storms that hit one after the other in Baca County. They would come in, he said, with boiling clouds that looked like canyon walls with caves in them rolling always toward you. The blackest part always hit first, then things would lighten up somewhat during the latter part of the storm, which often lasted two or three days. As a little boy, Bridge rather liked the dust storms: they blew the topsoil off and he could find all sorts of arrowheads and spear points. He especially remembers seeing a yucca plant standing straight up in the air on some six feet of exposed root, the surrounding dirt completely blown away.

Neufeldt's stories of 1950s dust storms provided an interesting comparison to the earlier storms. He remembers a couple of towering clouds of dust, but no rollers. The family lived a mile or so from the country schoolhouse, and several times the dust was so bad that school was dismissed. When this happened, he and his three brothers and sisters would hold hands, handkerchiefs over their faces, and walk in the grader ditch. They couldn't see a thing, but when they stumbled onto their driveway, they knew they were home.

Galen also told a story for John Ransom. It occurred
during the Dust Bowl days, but it's not about dust. It's a bit
gruesome, perhaps, but funny (in retrospect), and I'll draw
this chapter to a close with it. The Ransoms, like most Dust
Bowl (and other) farm families, were extremely poor, and
as Thanksgiving rolled around they were looking forward
to nothing but bacon and beans—that is, until John's grandmother, who lived in eastern Oklahoma, shipped them a
live turkey. It arrived a day or so before Thanksgiving and
the Ransoms didn't have a shed that would hold it, and no
refrigerator if they butchered it early, so they tied a rope
around one leg and hitched the bird to the fence. Unfortunately, the turkey flew around during the night and
landed in the pigpen. The next morning, all that was left
of their Thanksgiving dinner was the rope and one turkey
foot. That was more than some Dust Bowl farmers ended
up with!—*JH*

78. *Dust Pneumonia*

FOLKS EMERGING from hospital stays often remark that
disease is an equalizer felling the great as well as the
humble. This isn't exactly true. Some diseases are not at all
democratic.

Certain occupations are liable to certain maladies. Old-
time telegraphers suffered from a characteristic paralysis
of the hand and wrist. Modern laborers in packinghouses
have trouble with their hands because of doing repetitive
work in cold rooms.

Some of these occupational health hazards have a regional slant, which brings them into the domain of this
book. I recall that my father, a groundwater flood irri-
gator, had chronic problems with his knees. The reason
was obvious: he spent too much time wading around in
deadly cold water, pulling his feet from sucking mud with

every step. His trouble was similar to that of nineteenth-century mountain men who waded streams to check their traps during winter.

Other regional maladies derive not from a particular occupation but from the general environment. In southern Europe, because of something in the water, there is a goiter belt well known to medical scientists.

The outstanding examples of ailments stemming from the Great Plains environment are dust pneumonia and similar problems connected to the blowing dust of the 1930s and other droughty decades. In *An Empire of Dust* (recently reprinted by the University Press of Kansas as *Farming the Dust Bowl*), farmer-author Lawrence Svobida devotes a chapter to "Dust Dickness," wherein he describes his own lung problems, and another to "Tragedies of Dust," wherein he discusses efforts of doctors and hospitals to deal with dust pneumonia.

Dust pneumonia, Svobida explains, was the popular term for silicosis, or silica poisoning, resulting from taking dust into the lungs. It caused scar tissue to develop in the lungs and produced general anemia. Made the worse through simple clogging of the lungs by dirt, eventually it often led to tuberculosis or other fatal infections. During the year 1935, four hospitals in the Dust Bowl reported thirty-three deaths from this sort of respiratory disorder.

A student of mine from Salina, Kansas—Paul Sommers—has been interviewing people about health problems associated with the Dust Bowl. One doctor recalled that the respiratory problems of that time and place preceded sulfa drugs, which might have offered relief but which did not come into his hands until the early 1940s.

The remedy for one dust-related disorder, empyema, was to remove part of a rib and to insert a tube into the lung for drainage. This physician preferred that such surgery be done not in a local hospital, where epidemic disease and airborne grit threatened infection, but in the home, on the kitchen table.

I suppose a well-scrubbed kitchen was as good a place as any to do the surgery, but what a grotesque image that account adds to the album of this hard country's cultural history.—*TI*

79. *The Farm Pond*

IT'S REALLY NICE to drive through the Flint Hills in early summer and see the ponds all full. That, along with the bright green grass and the many wildflowers, is a sure sign that we've had a wet spring, and a wet spring means that despite thirsty cattle and evaporation there should be plenty of livestock water throughout pasture season, even if we have a drought.

The primary purpose of most farm or ranch ponds (or tanks, as they are called in Texas and other parts of the Southwest) is for watering cattle, but don't try to tell that to the young boys and girls who fish and swim in them. My sister and I learned to swim in a farm pond, one about a half-mile from our house, after having graduated from the horse tank at the windmill near the barn. It was a small pond but deep enough to have a diving board. What I liked best was the mud bottom, the smoothest, silkiest feeling my feet have ever known. At that age muddy or clear water made no difference to me; so long as it was wet and cool, it was good for swimming. We would often ride out after the milk cows early and swim before chores.

My earliest pond memories, however, are associated with fishing. I'm not much of a fisherman myself, but Grandpa Rice was and he loved to catch bullheads. Most farm ponds in this part of the country also have channel cat, bass, and crappie, especially in the many watershed dams that have been built in recent years.

Still, the major function of a farm pond is to water cattle. In the earliest days of settlement on the plains, livestock water was natural surface water: springs, creeks, or rivers. With the introduction of the windmill in the late 1800s, along with barbed wire, cattle could be pastured far from these natural sources of water. The windmill brought water to otherwise dry regions, but it also brought problems. For one thing, it required constant attention and checking. A hole in the tank or a broken jet rod could mean thirsty cattle in short order. For another, it also required wind. That is usually no problem on the plains, but if we do get a few days of calm, the result can be an expensive and very tiresome job of hauling water. Thus the pond, by creating a supply of water far from the natural sources, was a great labor and worry saver.

Today there are not so many windmills as there were a few decades past, not only because electric pumps have replaced them, but also because of the many farm ponds, ranch tanks, and watershed dams that have been erected in the last half-century. Either type of watering system, pond or windmill, has its own special advantages and disadvantages. While you can't fill a jug with cold drinking water from a farm pond, neither can you catch fish from a windmill.—*JH*

80. *The REA*

I NOTICED VARIOUS farm magazines publishing tributes to the Rural Electrification Administration on the occasion of its fiftieth anniversary in 1985. The creation of the Rural Electrification Administration in 1935 established a partnership between the federal government and local electrical cooperatives to extend electrification to rural America. This was important for rural dwellers across the United States, but nowhere more so than in the Great Plains.

The problem with electrical service on the plains was the tyranny of distance. Compared to more easterly sections of the United States, the Great Plains, because of their subhumid to semiarid climate, had a sparse rural population. Residences being far apart, the cost of providing electrification was high.

Prior to 1935, private power companies had been slow to extend lines into such disadvantagous rural areas as those of the plains. Such service required long lines to reach few homes. Many farmers, impatient for electricity, bought gasoline-powered generators.

During the presidential campaign of 1932, Franklin D. Roosevelt proposed federal aid for rural electrification. A promoter of public power, Morris L. Cooke, subsequently entered the Roosevelt administration, and when Roosevelt created the REA by executive order on May 11, 1935, he put Cooke in charge of it.

Cooke quickly decided that because of the reluctance of private power companies to serve rural residents, the only way to achieve rural electrification was to provide federal financial aid to local rural electrical cooperatives. The REA reduced the initial cost of rural service by extending low-interest, long-amortization loans to rural electrical cooperatives.

Work on rural electrification slowed during the 1940s, especially during the war, but soon picked up again. By the mid-1950s only the most remote American farms were without electricity. The plains, even with their sparse population, received electricity about the same time as the rest of the country.

Surveys showed that irons, radios, washing machines, and refrigerators were the first electrical devices that farm families sought after electrification. That goes to show just how much drudgery farm women bore before electrification and just how much they must have welcomed electrical appliances, as well as the contact with the outside world provided by radio.

The most visible result of electrification was the appearance of myriad home and yard lamps in the previously black rural night. This is something I think about often as I drive across the plains. How lonely it must have been for travelers in the region before electrification to have looked across the nighttime landscape and seen no glimmer of evidence of human habitation.

There are a number of events that residents of the plains may consider watersheds in their history—the Great Duster of April 14, 1935, comes to mind, as do the advents of the automobile and the tractor. Rural electrification, though, is different in one respect from these other things. Some of those other events were outright tragedies, and the remainder of them contained at least an element of ambivalence that might provoke nostalgia in the future. After the advent of tractors, for instance, there still were people who spoke with affection about horses or, as in the case of my Grandfather Dunekack, mules. But I have yet to meet anyone who questions the unmitigated good that came with rural electrification. Did you ever hear anyone say anything good about washing on a board or milking by kerosene lamp? I didn't think so.—TI

Part Six

MONUMENTS, RUINS, AND JUNK

81. *Grisly Monuments*

THE LOGGERHEAD SHRIKE, commonly known as the butcher bird, has adjusted handily to the presence of humans and their technology on the plains. The shrike, which feeds on large insects and small mammals, used to store its prey impaled on twigs and thorns. Today the butcher bird commonly sticks its victims onto the barbs of a wire fence.

The oddities of the shrike I will leave to the ornithologists, but I would like to know what motivates the human butcher birds that inhabit the plains. I began thinking along these lines while driving down Highway 99 just north of Hamilton, Kansas, where I noticed three large flathead catfish heads hanging from fenceposts. Suddenly thinking just how grotesque this common practice is, I stopped to take a few photographs. As I looked over the fish heads suspended from fence posts by pieces of baling wire, I noticed that stretching up the fence line from them was a row of shovelcat or paddlefish heads stuck onto posts, the paddles pointing downward.

I asked some people in the vicinity who had hung all those fishheads on fence posts, but no one seemed to know. What makes someone do such a thing? My first reaction is to say that it is someone's attempt to be remembered for his prowess as a fisherman. The hanger of fishheads may be akin to elk hunters who came home from the mountains with the heads of animals mounted on their vehicles or pheasant hunters who go back to work at IBP or Cessna the Monday after opening day with pheasant tail feathers stuck in their caps.

This explanation doesn't quite work, though, because the hangers of fish heads are anonymous. They achieve not fame but mystery. So now I think that the motivation of such exhibitionists must be the delight of creating a grisly, sinister monument that passers-by will notice and wonder about.

The same goes for those who hang coyote carcasses on fences. Since within the past decade the price of coyote fur has advanced markedly and since many coyote hunters prefer to sell the carcass with hide to hide buyers rather than skinning it out themselves, coyote carcasses are not much seen on fences anymore. In previous years such exhibitions, like fish heads, were common throughout the plains.

There were those who defended these disgusting displays by saying that hanging coyote carcasses on fences helped to keep other coyotes away and thereby protected sheep and calves from predators. I don't buy this. If the carcasses were meant to keep coyotes away, then the best place for them would have been on the back fences of pastures, not on the roadside fences. The coyotes, like the flatheads, more likely were hung for the unsettling effect upon passers-by.

In 1979 the legislature of Kansas came to the same conclusion that I have, that there is no particular reason for such grisly displays. That year the legislature declared it "unlawful for any person to publicly display the carcass of a coyote." Exempted were displays of skins and carcasses for commercial or educational purposes. To my knowledge no other state has passed such a law. I know from conversations with officials at the Texas Department of Parks and Wildlife that Texas has not.

An official at the Texas department described the hanging of catfish heads and coyote carcasses as "a rather traditional thing" and did not seem too disturbed about it. Does any practitioner of this sort of exhibition care to speak out and say what is the reason for it?—*TI*

82. *Folk Monuments to Hard Work*

WHEN I WROTE about people hanging catfish heads and coyote carcasses on fences, some folks thought those grisly monuments were a little grotesque. I have noticed another type of folk monument, a type that has deep sentiment behind it.

When you drive through the sandhills of Nebraska, unless you are transfixed by the wonderfully distant horizons, you will see worn-out cowboy boots slipped soles up onto the tops of fence posts. Sometimes there are just a pair, sometimes dozens along a fenceline. I have noticed the same thing in western Kansas and West Texas, but nowhere so much as in Nebraska.

In the same areas, and in the Osage Hills of Oklahoma and here in the Flint Hills of Kansas, you see another fence-row phenomenon: barbed wire balls. These are spheres, some three feet in diameter, made of discarded, rusty barbed wire. Like the boots, they are meant to be seen by people driving by.

As are the old stationary separators, or threshing machines, you see parked atop hills in those parts of the plains where they have hills. Although I've seen a few of these on the southern plains, looking from a distance like giant grasshoppers in some 1950s movie, they are most common in the Dakotas.

If you don't think these things are monuments, then consider that someone pulled that separator up the hill and unhitched it there. Someone decided that it ought to be seen by passers-by, seen not up close as in a museum, but from afar, so that it is not a complex combination of bolts and pulleys and sheet metal but rather a simple silhouette, a symbol.

What is the creator of such a folk monument trying to say? Any old-time small-grain farmer knows that the hardest season of the year was threshing time. He knows, but those young folks zipping by on the highway need to be reminded. The separator on the hill is a monument to hard work. Putting it on the hill elevates work. It's an endorsement of the work ethic.

What is the most continual and wearisome task of all cowboys since the enclosure of the open range? Fixing fence. So when, after years of maintaining a particular line of fence, the barbed wire, because of repeated burning or just rust, needs to be replaced, all that hard work ought to be remembered. Hence the barbed-wire balls. The usual thing to do with trash in pastures is to shove it into a gully, but somehow these brown spheres always end up on a rise, where they can be seen.

That brings us back to the boots on fence posts, another folk monument to hard work. The statement here is, "Well, I wore out another pair of boots working this danged place." The next year finds another pair alongside them, and after that the neighbors start sticking their old boots on the same fenceline.

A couple of years ago I was on a platform in Iowa alongside several scholars who hold endowed chairs or similar high academic positions. For some reason I checked out the footwear and counted one pair of boots (mine) and three identical pairs of brown wing tips. I had strayed out of my territory. You never see brown wing tips hanging on fenceposts.—*TI*

83. *Bent's Old Fort*

DURING THE SUMMER of 1985 our family visited one of the most famous of Great Plains landmarks, Bent's Old Fort, which has been reconstructed on its original site and is being operated by the National Park Service as a living museum. That means that all the furnishings are either authentic pieces from the period of the fort's original existence or they are accurate reproductions. In addition, people are hired to act out the roles of the original inhabitants—soldiers, trappers, traders, chambermaids.

Located a few miles from La Junta, Colorado, on the Arkansas River, Bent's Ford was a major trading center on the mountain branch of the Santa Fe Trail. The two Bent brothers, Charles and William, and their fellow St. Louisian, Ceran St. Vrain, had joined forces in the 1820s to engage in the fur trades. As trade goods moved back and forth to and from St. Louis and Santa Fe, the company making a profit on both ends, the partners decided to establish a fortified trading post in a location where they could both service the Santa Fe trade and also deal in the furs being taken by mountain men and Indians.

Although the fort was built on the American side of the Arkansas River, the brothers were nothing if not pragmatic in politics. Charles Bent married a Mexican woman and became a citizen of Mexico in order to gain trading concessions there, while William married Owl Woman, a Southern Cheyenne, in order to cement good relations with that influential tribe.

The fort itself, trapezoidal in shape and made of adobe and poles, was finished in 1834, rooms (surrounding an open courtyard) built into the outer walls. Some of these rooms were rented out to travelers, others were used for shops and storage, while still others served as living quarters for the Bents and their employees. A powder magazine, a billiards room and saloon, and a blacksmith shop (which, according to one visitor, was noisy day and night) were on the southwest corner, next to the adobe-walled corral.

An interesting feature of the corral is that the tops of the walls were planted solidly with cactus in order to keep the Indians from crawling over and stealing horses (a practice similar to setting broken glass in the tops of concrete walls today). In addition to Bent's Cheyenne in-laws, the trading post was also frequented by Kiowas, Arapahos, Utes, Apaches, and Comanches. The Comanches, however, were never allowed inside the fort, having instead to trade their furs one at a time through a window. Apparently William Bent, although he had been successful in getting the warring plains tribes to observe truces, never quite trusted the Comanches.

Bent's Old Fort reached its peak of success in the mid-1840s, then quickly declined. In 1846 the U.S. government comandeered it for use as a base during the Mexican War. Within a year white adventurers were pouring onto the plains, with resultant Indian warfare. In 1849 cholera struck the Indians with even greater force than the guns of the whites, and William Bent abandoned his old trading post. Either he or the Indians burned it to the ground.

Bent moved east fifty miles or so and built what is known as Bent's New Fort, which today is merely a pile of rubble amid the shortgrass. Thanks to the National Park Service, however, Bent's Old Fort stands again, giving modern plainsmen a brief glimpse into the past that many of us wish we could have lived.—*JH*

84. *The Deserted Farm*

ON MAY DAY 1985, I traveled out onto the High Plains and back into time. I was on my way to the home of Dean Davis, who had invited me to present a program on rodeo history for a community gathering. Dean lives north of Arriba, Colorado, a dozen miles or so from Linden, quite literally out in the middle of the wide-open spaces. I was a bit early so I decided to poke around the countryside a bit. To my mind there is nothing prettier than grassland, whether it's in my native Flint Hills or out on the High Plains. In addition to admiring the land itself, I like to look for windmills, cattle pens, silos—anything that shows how people have adapted to the land.

Or how they don't adapt. The High Plains, as well as the tallgrass country, has plenty of deserted farmsteads, which draw me like a magnet, and I pulled into one about twenty miles north of Arriba. At first it seemed a typical abandoned farm: people gone, but fields still under cultivation and outbuildings still in use for machine and grain storage. The house seemed to have been empty for several years.

There was a two-story pump house southeast of the barn, with a pump jack over the well where the windmill once stood. Two tanks in the corral stood about half full of water. The barn, most of its north wall fallen down, had held cattle earlier in the spring. A little low-roofed shed stood just east of the barn and north of the pump house. Possibly it was a playhouse: a child-size chair sat inside, along with a homemade toy made of a tobacco tin mounted on little wheels. A three-section wooden granary (facing east) lay north of the playhouse, still in use although currently empty. Nearby was a trailer for hauling loaf-stacked hay.

A chicken house, facing south and running longways east and west, stood on the northern perimeter of the improvements. It was divided into three distinct sections and had three or four doors, most of them ajar. I don't know how long it had been without chickens, but on this warm day it still carried their smell. It was being used for storage: some fifty-gallon oil drums, parts of an old washing machine, some canvas slats off an old combine, other odds and ends. Two sacks of wheat had been placed on barrels to keep them from the rats, a futile effort. Both had been chewed open, one rat scurrying away as I looked inside. There was a date, 1941, marked into the step, but the building looked older; perhaps the concrete had been added later. A machine shed, southeast of the chicken house, had the appearance of a small barn but had been used for storing tractors or cars. The big wooden swinging doors on the southeast corner were held shut by wooden bars, a 1954 car tag bent around one of the bar holders for added strength.

About eighty feet southwest of the house was the outhouse, leaning rather sharply to the southwest, a single-holer with the wooden-tunnel ventilation system often found in country school outhouses. A clothesline, looping but still solid enough to support a midsized load of wash, stood just west of the outhouse.

Scattered throughout the yard and the rest of the farmstead were some dead or dying Chinese elms, the tree that made shade possible on the High Plains. Electric lines leading into the house and to the pump jack stood as mute tes-

timony to the pervasiveness of the rural electrification program begun half a century ago.

The house itself, however, was the most interesting
piece of vernacular architecture on the place.—*JH*

85. *The Sod House*

IN THE LAST chapter I described an abandoned farmstead
on the High Plains near Linden, Colorado. Of the various
structures on the place, the house itself, surrounded by
woven-wire fence, was the most intriguing building. It had
been built in two parts at two different times and at a casual glance appeared to be composed of a newer wooden
structure joined to an older stucco house. The stucco part,
on the west side, ran north and south and was about twelve
by twenty feet. The roof was low and flat and held down
by guy wires, two of them veeing out from each corner.
There was no window or door on the north, but there was
a small tin-roofed lean-to sloping down from the northeast
corner. The two windows on the west were framed by
wooden trellises, set out a couple of feet from and attached
to the house. Obviously they had once held vines that had
helped to screen out the High Plains sun.

As I approached, I saw that the stucco was actually a
veneer of concrete, about two inches thick, that had pulled
away from the bottom of the window, revealing an example of that classic of Great Plains architecture—the sod
house. The south side of the house had two small windows
and a door. Above and to the east of the door there was
no concrete veneer, nor did there appear ever to have
been any. Perhaps weathering was not so bad from the
southeast and this part of the house had not needed the
extra protection. The concrete veneer itself was rather
crudely formed, with board marks ranging from eight to
twelve inches in width visible where the wet concrete had
been poured. There appeared to have been some attempt

to smooth out the concrete on the west side of the house, less obvious an effort on the north.

Peering through one of the windows, I could see that the east wall had begun to cave in. Several holes were visible in the burrow-riddled sod; the smell of raccoons was strong in the air. The two portions of the house were attached along the east wall of the soddy, the frame part undoubtedly added on when the inhabitants had become more financially secure. This part of the house, also about twelve by twenty feet, ran east and west and had a higher and more steeply pitched roof than the sod house. An enclosed sun porch ran the full south length of the three-room wooden addition. The two east rooms appeared to be small bedrooms, the other a living room.

The sod portion also appeared to have three rooms, probably two bedrooms to the north and a kitchen-living area in the south half. On the north side of the wooden house was a storm cellar with no outside door; it could be entered only from the northeast bedroom. The storm cellar may have been added at the time the wooden annex was built, but more probably, it seems to me, considering the typical plains respect for violent weather, it was already dug and simply incorporated into the new addition as it was being built. Among the old furniture, mattresses, jars, and other debris lying around the sun porch was a calendar from 1962.

It is difficult to describe the feelings I had as I got into my car and pulled out of the driveway, heading for the Davis ranch. Some nostalgia, some poignance, intense curiosity about the people who had built, then abandoned, this place. It may be a cliché, but if only those walls could have talked!

The historical facts could be checked, of course, but I have decided not to do that research. Perhaps the strongest feeling I had that day was one of affinity with the plains pioneers, of having shared in their lives as they built that sod house, sought its warmth in the icy plains winters, its cool in the searing Augusts. I really don't want or need any disillusioning facts to interfere with this picture in my mind, to destroy this sense of oneness with all the people who built sod houses.—*JH*

86. *Pyramids of the Plains*

DON WORSTER'S BOOK *Dust Bowl*, published in 1979, won the Bancroft Prize, which identifies it as a superb work of history. Certain passages in it troubled me, though. In them Worster says that the southern plains were settled so hastily, and the settlements were so unstable, that they had no culture at all.

It is typical for people to misunderstand the culture of the plains, because they don't reckon with how the large scale and high risk typical of any enterprise in the region affect the ways people think and behave. The people of the plains largely understand the facts that Carl Kraenzel put into his book *The Great Plains in Transition:* mobility and flexibility, the avoidance of fixed capital, are the keys to survival. Mobility and flexibility are the culture of the plains, the culture of cattle drives, wheat harvesting, and wildcatting, but these traits are misinterpreted by outsiders as transitoriness and superficiality.

The way we live ought to inspire humility, however. Plains Indians moved across the landscape and left hardly a mark on it. We think that we are different, that we effect great and permanent changes, but I'm not so sure. Houses, barns, schools, churches, whole towns, even cemeteries— how quickly they have disappeared under tillage during the past generation as abandonment of family farms has vacated the landscape.

All these center pivots that make us think we can create the garden of the world with underground rain—they won't last that long, historically speaking. We bulldoze out our precious groves and windbreaks so the circles can pivot, forgetting that a previous generation believed those trees were the keys to the garden. And the folks who planted those trees, thinking that they might thereby modify the climate, did so because they had learned to their grief that rain did not follow the plow, as they had been told.

When railroads building across the plains missed existing towns, the residents moved the towns to the railroads. Now that truck transport has replaced rail shipping, we take up the tracks. The Interstate Highway System in turn has taken away the trade of countless towns—they closed the last remaining stretch of old Route 66 a few years ago—so now the merchants move out onto the Interstate exchanges, where we find commercial clusters every bit as sad and puffed up as the false fronts of the settlement era.

If this is the way we live, then what marks are we going to leave on the landscape for another generation's archaeologists? I have just about concluded that what we are going to leave behind is our mistakes: the cases where we forgot the facts of life in our region, got carried away, and erected something so solid, costly, and permanent that all who came after us had to go around it.

What started me thinking in this fashion was teaching a course in the folklore of the Great Plains, concentrating on what academics call "material culture," meaning the physical objects and structures that people use in their everyday lives. The students and I, in the course of some fieldwork, decided that there is at least one type of farm structure that constitutes such a grand mistake that it will endure to be called by future generations the pyramids of the plains. So it's worth writing about.—*TI*

87. *Concrete Silos*

THE PYRAMIDS of the plains are not houses of commerce, seats of government, or temples of worship, but simple concrete silos. I mean the type of poured concrete, not concrete staves. The stave type is more common and less permanent; it's relatively easy to take down when it has outlived its usefulness. The poured-concrete type, or "monolithic," as agricultural engineers used to call it, is less common, but it's there forever, unless you have some dynamite handy. Better just go around it.

It takes two things to appreciate poured-concrete silos properly. The first is the willingness to stop your car, go out in a field or farmstead, and converse with one. Stand close enough to be dwarfed by it; stick your head in a window; run your hands around the rough walls.

If that feeling stirs you, then you're ready for the second step, which is to learn the history of these great cylinders. They resulted from a coincidence between the early phase of the silo craze on the plains, from the late 1890s to about World War I, and the climax of development in the American cement industry, a major cause of which was the discovery of cheap energy—natural gas—in the eastern sectors of Texas, Oklahoma, and Kansas. Farmers during this time applied the relatively inexpensive concrete to many farm uses, but especially silos.

Building a monolithic concrete silo was no task to embark upon lightly. In addition to material (cement and sand, perhaps mixed with gravel or crushed stone), the task required know-how and hard labor applied over many days. Concrete silo walls were poured in layers of some thirty-three inches that had to dry for at least five hours. The common practice was to pour a layer each day. (The rings visible around old monolithic concrete silos mark where one day's work left off and another's began.) Neighbors helped and received help in return, using the same forms. That's why you generally find poured-concrete silos in neighborhood groups.

Progress was slow, but solid and visible. The workers first built the forms, sometimes of wood flooring, more often of 36-inch-wide sheet metal. Arrangements of templates and wedges held the inside form out against the concrete; templates and bolts tightened the outside form in. Within a circular concrete foundation the workers raised a central pole and scaffolding around the pole. On the foundation they raised the walls, "working them up with the forms," as they said.

Old agricultural bulletins describe this process of moving up the forms as simple and straightforward. It could not have been so. The problems of loosening the stuck forms, pulling them up, getting them level, and keeping them plumb, not to mention raising the concrete to fill them, are more than I want to think about. Plus you had to arrange the rods and hog-wire reinforcement inside the forms, work around the window forms, and keep the concrete moist while it cured.

I suspect that most monolithic concrete silos on the plains were bad investments. They were twice as expensive as wood-stave silos, and although they lasted forever, hardly any were used much longer than the wooden ones were. Apparently impractical, as viewed in retrospect, they were in their time expressions of confidence in the future of the country. Since most of them now are tombstones for abandoned farmsteads, it is only proper respect to let them stand.—*TI*

88. *Observations on Silos*

IN OUR TRIPS together here and there around the plains I have noticed that Tom, reared on a wheat farm and trained as an agricultural historian, sees everything there is to see on a farmstead, while my own vision tends to be more selective, limited to things bovine and equine both by my background and by academic interest. I had never, for example, paid much attention to silos until Tom wrote about their role as unintentional monuments to our agricultural heritage, about how they are every bit as evocative in their way as ruined castles are in theirs. Now I can

hardly drive anywhere without scouring the skyline for cy-
lindrical shapes—or without pulling into every farmyard
that has an unusual silo.

As is generally the case with ignorance, I had thought
that one silo was pretty much like another, except for the
big enclosed blue Harvestore stainless-steel models that began popping up a few years past. (They, and a few enclosed concrete silos, are about the only upright silos still
used; most ensilage today is stored in trenches.) I have
found, however, that silos have been built in a variety of
sizes and with a variety of materials: wood, brick, native
stone, sheet metal, ceramic tile (in a wide assortment of colors and sizes), concrete block (some regular, some slightly
curved), concrete stave (which look something like pieces
from a jigsaw puzzle), and poured concrete. Homemade
silos were sometimes constructed of snow fence or were
fashioned by stacking grain sorghum in a tall, open circle,
butts to the inside, and then blowing the chopped feed into
the center.

Considering that the majority of silos on the plains have
not been used for at least a quarter of a century, many
twice that long, it might at first seem a bit surprising that so
many are still standing, and indeed most of the wooden
and many of the metal ones have been torn down for salvage. But what do you—or, more precisely, what *can* you—
do with a concrete or a tile silo when it is no longer used
for storing ensilage? Well, there are people who will dis-
assemble concrete-stave silos, then use the interlocking
pieces to create a paved driveway or sidewalk. And I suppose that a silo could be dynamited or bulldozed and the
rubble used for fill—a rather expensive and dangerous
method for obtaining not very much of a not very scarce
commodity.

But if you don't tear them down, then what? Silos, especially covered ones, can be used for storing other farm
products (such as hay or grain), but the very structural design that makes a silo so practical for ensilage makes it a

cumbersome storage shed. There have been other uses. An old ceramic-tile silo on the outskirts of Emporia is used by its owner as a trash burner, one that will take years and years to fill with ash and debris. I have been told of a high school biology teacher in Harper County, Kansas, who collected and sold wildlife to schools and laboratories; he used an abandoned silo as a herpetorium—a genuine snake pit. I have seen photographs of a silo that was converted into a house—a circular staircase winding up through three or four false floors to a large, round penthouse built onto and hanging out over the top. It had the appearance of a lighthouse looking out onto a wheat field instead of an ocean. Here in Emporia an enterprising beer distributor has had a concrete-stave silo painted to replicate a giant can of Coors, a real attention getter for drivers whizzing along the Kansas Turnpike.

As Tom has noted, however, most unused silos today stand in varying states of ruin, monuments to an agricultural reality that no longer obtains. There is no more eloquent statement of capability turned anachronistic, of function rendered archaic, than the branches of a tree growing out and over the top of a still-solid but obviously long-abandoned silo.—*JH*

89. *Building Silos*

ENSILAGE MUST HAVE BEEN thought the feed of the future earlier in this century, judging from the number of unused silos now dotting the countryside. Most of these surviving structures (which run the gamut from good as new to crumbling apart) had commercial, not folk, origins. Some were built by the farmer from materials purchased from a dealer or according to plans obtained from the local extension office, while others were erected by professional builders. One usually sees clusters of like silos in a

particular area; monolithic poured concrete will predomi-
nate in one neighborhood, for instance, ceramic tile in another, concrete stave with distinctive paint designs in yet
another—evidence of the persuasiveness of some now-
forgotten salesman.

Tom has described in an earlier chapter the difficulty
and complication of building a one-piece (i.e., monolithic)
concrete silo. These silos can easily be detected as you drive
through the countryside because of the way they were
poured—a separate three-foot layer of concrete per day.
Each ring has a slightly different color and texture, reflect-
ing the distinct if slight differences in each day's batch of
concrete and weather conditions.

In addition to these "layered" silos I have seen monolithic concrete silos that lack the rings, that give the appearance of having been poured in a single setting, even though
they may have taken many days to construct. This type of
silo, as nearly as I have been able to determine, was built by
pouring and plastering the "mud" into place around a
framework of wood and reinforcement rods.

Loretta Sawin of Waterville, Kansas, has sent me some
pictures of a silo built by her father in 1912 near the small
town of Barnes. This silo (at twenty-two feet eight inches
by fifty feet) was, according to the caption on two old picture postcards, the "largest silo in the state." It was constructed "on the farm of C. J. Solt . . . by Cullinan and
Sawin, Barnes, Kansas, of Fredonia Cement. See us for Si-
loes." One of the postcards shows the wooden frame being
built (Sawin's part of the job; he was a carpenter), the other
the silo nearing completion with the concrete in place but
the wooden scaffolding not yet removed. "It is interesting
to me," Miss Sawin wrote, "that the silo is still standing, the
name and date still able to be read." The photograph she
took in October 1986 shows a structure as solid now as the
day it was built. It also reveals that the top half of the silo is
slightly darker in color than the bottom half, indicating
that once the framework was in place the workers were
able to run the concrete in only two days.

I haven't had a chance to talk to any old-time silo contractors, but I did hear from J. R. Allen of Ottawa, Kansas, about his experiences in helping to erect concrete-stave silos one summer while he was still in high school. It was around 1930 and after working on the silo being built on the home place, he hired out to the contractor to build four more. As he recalls there were a number of other boys helping and they would stand on the ladder inside the chute and hand up the heavy concrete staves one after the other. Mr. Allen said that if a stave broke as it was being passed up, whoever had it would shout a warning, then drop it down the chute: "We held our stomachs in as it went past." I asked if the men on top placing the staves worked from a scaffold or from the top of the silo as it grew taller. Mr. Allen didn't remember: "We didn't have time to look up."

Whatever the material used for construction, building silos was hard work.—*JH*

90. *Wooden Silos*

GENERALLY SPEAKING, ruins of stone are more impressive, more colorful than those of wood. A small, abandoned frame house rotting away is an eyesore, while a structure of similar size and state of disrepair but made of native stone or of brick maintains an air of poignance—of elegance ruined, perhaps, but elegance nonetheless. On the other hand, it seems to me, the wooden silo is an exception to this rule. Perhaps I find them attractive because wooden silos, once as plentiful as those of concrete or tile, are now rare, but I honestly think their construction is more aesthetically pleasing than that of the concrete silo.

Wooden silos proliferated in the early years of this century. They came in two general types: stave (a round silo made of tongue-in-groove two-inch lumber, often cyprus to forestall rot, installed vertically on a concrete base) or timber crib (usually octagonal with two-by-fours or two-by-sixes stacked horizontally, again on concrete). Frank Frey, reared near Hymer in northern Chase County, Kansas, showed me a photograph of the wooden-stave "John Deere" silo on the home place. It was called that, he said, because his father bought the materials (lumber, clamps, and instructions) from the John Deere company, which evidently had a franchise of some sort. And I know that there were at least two similar silos in a Midland, Texas, feedlot in 1926 because I have seen a photograph showing their construction.

It is doubtful that these two silos still stand; I know that the Frey silo no longer exists. Concrete or tile silos, as remarked in earlier chapters, have become the Great Plains version of pyramids or castles, abandoned but majestic ruins, while few wooden silos have survived to the present time. One reason is that the wooden silo was more susceptible than concrete or tile to such natural disasters as fire or wind. More important, though, was economic necessity; good two-inch lumber is simply too valuable a commodity to escape salvage. Breathes there a farmer or rancher with purse so full that he would go out and buy new lumber for a tool shed, hog shelter, or cattle pen when he has perfectly good thirty-foot boards just standing there in that old silo? I saw some of these cypress boards in a machine shed on the Wayne Brant farm near Thayer, Kansas, still waiting to be used decades after the silo had been dismantled.

Lately, as my eye has become more attuned to round wooden buildings on farmsteads, I have learned of another fate that befell wooden silos: they were cut down and converted into smaller sheds. J. R. Allen of Ottawa, Kansas, has a wooden-stave shed, about ten or twelve feet high and fourteen feet in diameter, in his barn lot. It was carved from a thirty-foot silo in the early 1930s and the rest of the lumber sold. It held up to twelve hundred bushels of corn, although recently it has been used only for keeping a few bales of hay. Ed Broz of rural Marion County has a wooden-stave granary on his farm, made in the early 1930s from a 36-foot-tall silo. The silo, he recalls, didn't protect feed as well as did concrete; air seeped in where the boards met, and the silage would dry out for several inches into the interior. Arza Fogle of Williamsburg, Kansas, cut his silo in two and made it into a chicken house and a tool shed. An octagonal timber-crib silo on the W. A. Bolz farm near Reading, Kansas, built around 1915, was later cut down into two tool sheds, one retaining the original roof, the other with a flat tin roof sloping to the north.

Although not many wooden silos still stand, those that do add both to the beauty and to the poignance of the Great Plains landscape.—*JH*

91. *C. P. Short's Wooden Silo*

IN JANUARY 1987 I was headed west on U.S. 160 about a mile or two east of Harper, Kansas, when I caught a glimpse of a familiar-looking shape out of the corner of my eye—sure enough, a wooden silo. I turned into the farmyard and, as is often the case in instances such as this, I found not only a rare Great Plains agricultural relic but also some warm hospitality and an entertaining human story.

C. P. (Clarice) Short answered my knock on the back door of the house and ushered me in to talk to his wife, Alice, whose father had built the silo sometime after he bought the farm ground in 1906. The silo was a beauty, weathered heavily enough to be picturesque but still sturdy, a roofed, octagonal, timber-crib model with some of the original shiplap siding on the outside. A few scraps of tar paper still clung to the interior. It was constructed, I was told, of precut two-by-fours, each around six feet long, the ends nailed together with sixteen-penny nails: one ton of sixteen-penny nails, to be exact. Originally it stood con-

nected to a cattle shed and a barn so that the stored feed
could be fed more easily. Today it stands alone.

In the 1930s the silo, no longer used for ensilage, was
converted into a grain elevator. Mr. Short divided the
structure into thirds, installing three floors (concrete at
the base and two wooden false floors, each supported by
oak four-by-four sills purchased from a trucker passing
through from the Ozarks) and a foot-square chute up the
middle with openings for letting out the grain. On the
north side he put in a concrete dump pit and installed a
belt-and-cup lift powered by an electric motor mounted inside the peak of the roof. The capacity, he told me, must
have been just under four thousand bushels, because one
of the wooden floors broke when he put that much in,
spilling wheat into the adjoining shed. After that he no
longer used it as a granary and later tore out the insides.
Small amounts of maize and flax have occasionally been
kept on the concrete floor in the intervening years, but for
the most part it has stood idle. Why wasn't it torn down, I
asked, as has happened to so many others? Because, he
said, it's a reminder of earlier days. In fact, he would even
like to have it restored if the expense weren't so great.

I found that this appreciation for beauty was typical of
the Shorts, both of whom have led interesting lives. Both
write poetry and use their poems in constructing their own
greeting cards, which they send to friends on appropriate
occasions and which they have sold (five hundred in one
day is their record) at hobby shows when snowbirding in
Texas a few years ago. Both have taught school (attending
my own university for their certificates back in the 1920s),
Clarice for only a couple of years. Alice, though, taught
Latin and Spanish in Kingman and Harper counties for
nearly half a century, then taught migrant-worker children
while wintering in Texas.

Clarice, after a couple of years in the classroom, went to
Elgin, Illinois, to learn the watch-repair business, working
at shops in Kingman, Hutchinson, and Topeka before

opening his own jewelry store in Harper in 1927, starting
with $350 and his tools. He began farming in 1942 and
then, with his sons, branched out into the implement business. Born in 1900 (I would have guessed him younger),
he still maintains an interest in both enterprises—and in
poetry and history and old wooden silos.—*JH*

92. *Cattle Pens*

APPARENTLY WHEN Tom drives along the highways of the
Great Plains, he sees forty-foot snakes, giant armadillos,
Bigfoots (Bigfeet?), and other such oddities. At least he
does a lot of writing about them. Me? The best I can do is
an occasional jackrabbit or a pheasant snaking through the
grass at the side of the road. My chief method of making
the miles go faster is to look for interesting man-made
structures—unusual cattle guards or hay barns or silos.
Among my favorite mile-passers are the many sets of cattle
pens scattered throughout the plains.

You can tell much about an operation—and about local
conditions—by looking at a set of pens. On the High Plains
of Colorado or New Mexico, for instance, pens are often
made of lodgepole pine hauled in from the mountains,
while in West Texas or the Oklahoma Panhandle heavy
pipe (from the local oil or gas fields) is a favored material.
Solidly built, well-maintained pens (especially if they in-
clude a set of scales and a scale house) indicate a pros-
perous operation. Rundown pens—broken boards, bent
pipe, sagging wire—suggest that the owner isn't doing so
well financially. Or that he has acquired some portable
pens and has stopped maintaining the permanent ones.

One can also trace changes in the technology of the
cattle industry by looking at pens. Earlier in this century
many pens were designed chiefly for working cattle—
branding, dehorning, weaning. Sometimes market steers

were sorted in these pens before being driven to railroad stockyards for weighing and shipping. Then, with the big semitrailer cattle trucks, cattle pens acquired loading chutes. More recently the semi has given way to the gooseneck trailer, and the loading ramps have been lowered four or five feet.

Even more interesting to me than the well-made board or pipe pens are the homemade ones, examples of folk ingenuity. Ranchers with access to military surplus, for instance, have built some solid pens out of World War II landing mats. The most unusual pens I've seen were made entirely of old bedsprings. Not very pretty, but cheap and effective.

I also like to look at the architecture of cattle pens: the length and shape of the lead-in wing, the arrangement and size of individual pens, the nature of the building materials, the reinforcement of the sides (where the cattle push against them), the position of the scales and loading chute. Somewhere there is probably an ideal set of pens, but most ranchers are still trying to decide just what that ideal is. I don't think that I've ever seen two sets that were exactly alike.

I mentioned portable pens earlier. Recently someone told me about meeting a set of pens on a country road. The pens were set up with a wheel on each side and were being pulled by a tractor. Inside were a dozen or so cows and calves being taken from winter quarters to summer pasture. That's a slick idea, but not a new one. C. W. Ackermann, an old-time trail driver from San Antonio, recorded his experiences in shipping cattle from the Texas Gulf Coast in the 1860s. The area had many wooden-pole cattle pens, he noted, including one set (built by an Irishman) that was mounted on rollers. Thus any cattle trying to stampede would move the pens with them instead of breaking through. According to Ackermann, the pens would sometimes be fifty yards away from where they had been the night before, but the cattle were still inside.—*JH*

93. *Dump Rakes*

THE EARLIEST JOB I remember having in the hay field, other than catching horseflies off the stacker mules or carrying a fresh jug of water from the windmill to the haystack, was raking hay. In the early 1950s we bought a used side-delivery rake to pull behind the tractor in order to make neat, even rows for our new Allis baler. Loose-stacking hay with a go-devil and a jayhawk stacker, however, had required no such fancy, expensive equipment. Our horse-drawn dump rake was more than adequate to create the parallel windrows that gave geometric shape to the field and a sense of order to the mown grass.

Sometimes called a sulky rake because of its superficial resemblance to the vehicle pulled by harness-racing horses, the dump rake was an ingenious device that scraped hay together immeasurably faster than could a man and a pitchfork. These rakes varied in width (ours was probably a ten- or twelve-foot model) and were composed of an angle-iron frame with two large steel wheels on each end; a tongue, to which to hitch the mules, extending at a right angle from the middle of the rake (straight out from the iron seat where the driver sat); and a series of long, curved, spring-steel teeth (directly under and to the right and left of the driver) that gathered up the hay as the rake was driven across the field.

The driver stepped on a foot pedal to raise the teeth and dump the hay when the "barrel" of the rake was full. (Let it get too full and it sometimes took a pretty good kick to get it dumped.) On subsequent trips across the field you tripped the rake where you had dumped a load before, thereby creating a reasonably straight windrow for the go-devil to travel down.

I don't recall any problems with our rake (other than my lacking a sufficient motivational vocabulary if Andy happened to be one of the mules hitched to it), but the potential for serious mishaps was definitely there. If the driver would happen to fall in front of the teeth, for instance, he could be in for a real spin around the field. Recently I talked to some retired farmers at Hillsboro, Kansas, who told of exciting rides with runaway rake teams. One man was thrown backwards off the rake just as the team hit a gully (they had first hit a nest of bumblebees). A woman told me about once falling in front of the rake, but luckily she had hit the pedal as she went off and the teeth tripped just as she hit the ground, leaving her untouched. The brother of another informant was not so lucky; he carries several leg scars to remind him of his misadventure.

One of the last jobs in the hay field was raking the "scatterin's," the hay that had been left by the go-devil as it moved down the windrow; we tried to get every last forkful from the field. Today's machines that mow and windrow in one operation are unquestionably efficient as far as labor is concerned, but the loose hay one often sees around the big round bales makes me want to get out into the fields and rake scatterin's.—*JH*

94. *Old Dump Rakes*

I SUPPOSE that there are a few horse-drawn dump rakes still being used in the old-fashioned way, either by farmers who keep draft horses for a hobby or in living-history demonstrations of how things used to be done, but I think that it has been twenty-five years since we last used our rake, and then we had to pull it by hitching one of the saddle horses alongside the only broke mule we had at the time. Today our dump rake sits east of a windbreak on the home place, along with some other unused machinery.

Other people have been more creative with their abandoned rakes. The iron wheels, for instance, I have seen made into gates or panels for loading pens. The spokes had been cut at the hub, the rim straightened into a line, then matched with another wheel similarly cut and the spoke ends welded together. It's not the prettiest gate in the world, but with some braces and properly hung it's effective and much cheaper than one from WW or Powder River.

Other people have succumbed to the folk urge to transform junk into art. Rake teeth, with their semicircular arc and a small double-circle twist at the top to make them springy, seem to be especially prized by folk artists. I have seen rake teeth worked into mailbox supports, but the major use seems to be in conjunction with flowers, such as a circle of teeth arched over an old tractor tire made into a flower bed. The most attractive arrangement I have seen was made of a rake wheel welded about five feet above the ground onto a pipe post. A number of rake teeth had been spaced around the wheel, flower pots hanging from the end of each gracefully curving tooth.

At least one person, Rusty Longhofer, an implement dealer from Marion, Kansas, has become a collector of dump rakes. He didn't set out to become a collector, he told me, but he bought a few at farm sales several years ago, then bought a few more, and now he has several dozen (many of them parked in a row in a pasture bordering the highway just east of town)—and a reputation.

One man looking for a rake to buy told Rusty that when he had asked an implement dealer in Wichita about one he was told to go to Marion. The next dealer told him the same thing, so he gave up looking in Wichita and immediately headed to Marion. Other people have bought rakes at sales, some over a hundred miles away, and brought them to Longhofer, knowing he would buy them without haggling.

Longhofer has seen rakes as small as eight feet (used, he believes, in the smaller hay fields in states east of the plains) and as large as fourteen, but most are ten to twelve feet wide. And how is the market for dump rakes? Longhofer said that when he first started, five dollars was a typical price at a farm auction. Today a rake will often bring twenty or twenty-five dollars. In the future? Who knows. As Longhofer says, "they aren't making them any-more."—*JH*

95. *A Jumbo Windmill*

HERE IS A LETTER I wrote to T. Lindsay Baker, of Canyon, Texas, the world's foremost authority on windmills.

Dear Lindsay:

It was the Lord's own design that this plains country should be gridded with section roads, so that you and I could cruise the countryside looking for odd contraptions and not get lost. That's how I spotted, just southwest of Bushton, in Rice County, Kansas, a jumbo windmill.

By calling it a "jumbo," I'm borrowing a term from Erwin Hinckley Barbour, who wrote the pioneering documents on homemade windmills (*The Homemade Windmills of Nebraska*, 1899, and *Wells and Windmills in Nebraska*, 1899). This fellow Barbour was kin to us, don't you think? Eccentric—devoting his career to documenting and photographing homely-but-effective devices for raising water. And radical—advancing, in print, the notion that ordinary folks might come up with ideas and inventions better suited to their needs than the products of industry and science. He must have lived in tolerant times.

Somehow, during the mid-1940s, the spirit of E. H. Barbour was visited upon William Oberle of Rice County. It moved him to set four posts in a six-by-six-foot square and then nail odd boards, one-inch and two-inch, onto the posts to form an open-topped box five and one-half feet high.

Into holes bored through the uppermost boards Oberle inserted a shaft of one-and-one-quarter-inch pipe. Two-by-four arms were attached perpendicular to the shaft and braced with short two-by-fours, angle-iron, and strap-iron. One-inch boards nailed to these arms composed four paddles. So the top of the box looked like the rear end of a paddle-wheel riverboat.

To the end of the shaft, outside the box, directly over a well, Oberle welded the pitman crank from an old binder or header. This converted the circular motion of the shaft, driven by wind on the paddles, into the rectilinear motion needed to draw water.

I'm not sure that Oberle called his windmill a jumbo, but that's what he had, all right. It meets what seem to me to be the three essential characteristics of the homemade windmill. First, it's cheap, built mainly of junk and scrap. Second, it's effective, if not efficient. I talked to Wessel Ringwald of Ellinwood, who later had cattle in the pasture; he thinks he ran the windmill in 1980 or so, and it still supplied water dependably. Third, it's ugly as mud.

The builder's son, William, lives in Claflin. He doesn't know for sure where his father got the idea for the jumbo, but believes he saw one like it in western Kansas.

Whoever last used the jumbo tied one of the paddles to one of the posts with a piece of baling wire, so the mill probably has not turned since 1980, and a box-elder tree is growing inside the box. Cattle in the pasture now water from a dugout in the slough.

I'll be back in touch. I've spotted another homemade job, this one a merry-go-round mill, down on the Oklahoma line.—*TI*

96. *A Merry-Go-Round Windmill*

I'M WRITING again to Lindsay Baker, the windmill man in Canyon.

Dear Lindsay:

Sometimes you don't have to stray far from the main road to find a monument to old-time folk technology. On the east side of Interstate 35, just north of the Kansas-Oklahoma line, maybe a hundred yards south of the

Arkansas City–Highway 166 interchange, are the remains of a home-made merry-go-round windmill.

Here again I'm adopting a term coined by E. H. Barbour, the Nebraska windmiller from the turn of the century— "merry-go-round" meaning that the windmill turns in a circle in a horizontal plane, not standing up and facing the wind. None of Barbour's windmills looked much like this one I'm talking about, but the principle is the same.

With a little help from the *Arkansas City Traveler* I got in touch with Floyd and Dixie Mobray, who own and live on the land the mill is on, and they led me also to Everett and Elsie Hamilton, previous owners.

An associate of Mr. Hamilton tells me he "is now 90 years old, walks with crutches but still rides a bicycle around town," the town being Wellington, Kansas. It was he who in 1937 put in the well, with some financing from one federal government program or another, and built the windmill. The parts he used were hedge posts and junk from a junkyard; the most expensive part was a Model T differential, which cost him $1.00.

The windmill sits atop two pairs of posts set in a square, with two iron rails connecting the tops of the individual posts in the pairs. The Model T differential and axle are attached to the rails, with the wheels bolted to the rails, the differential located in the middle of the square of posts (but about six feet off the ground), and the drive shaft pointing straight up from the differential.

Atop the drive shaft are mounted two tapered two-by-fours in a cross. These are the rotor-arms of the merry-go-round. At their ends are four steel half-barrels, the barrels having been cut in half lengthways. These half-barrels are the fans that catch the wind and turn the mill. Or used to. It turned counter-clockwise, viewed from below. A pitman welded on one end of the Model T axle converted the motion to pump the hand-pump situated below it.

To stop the mill, you wired one of the drum-halves to a fifth hedge post set at the perimeter of the circle of motion. To keep it going, you just greased it once in a while.

Hamilton also replaced the original barrels in 1957 or so. The ones on it now are fairly small, maybe twenty-gallon; larger ones, Hamilton says, pumped more water than he needed for the thirty or so cattle in the pasture. The mill is inoperable now, with two of the barrels fallen off, but Floyd Mobray says he ran it after he bought the place in 1972.

There might be more of these cheap, homely, effective contraptions in the vicinity. Hamilton says he got the general idea for this one when he observed one like it from a distance, and he also built three others. It would be a sight to see one of them spinning.—*TI*

97. *Windwagons*

THE WIND HAS BLOWN with its usual vernal gusto during the spring of 1986, as I am sure it has throughout the Great Plains. Dodge City, I have heard, not Chicago, is America's true windy city, the municipality with the highest average wind velocity. I experienced some real wind power a couple of weeks ago while tarring down flapping shingles and watching the neighbor's wind generator spinning, and it got me to thinking about earlier experiments to harness this powerful force.

I recall reading in grade school about Windwagon Smith, a fictional entrepreneur who sailed into Westport in the 1850s and talked the locals into financing a literal prairie schooner so that they could monopolize the Santa Fe trade. He figured that his windwagon, carrying both passengers and freight, could make the Santa Fe trip in a week, only a tenth of the normal time. Unfortunately, the steering mechanism broke on the maiden voyage and the last anyone ever saw of Windwagon Smith, he was scudding backwards toward Council Grove faster than a horse could run.

Wilbur Schramm probably based his story of Wind-

wagon Smith on the exploits of a man named Thomas
from Independence, Missouri, who was planning to travel
the Santa Fe Trail to Bent's Fort in a wind-powered wagon
as early as 1846. Manufacturing his machine took longer
than expected, however, and it was not until 1853 that
Thomas left Westport on a trial run of a hundred miles. A
larger wagon launched some time later wrecked, costing
Thomas both his financial backers and his plans for a fleet
of windwagons offering regular mail and freight service
over the Santa Fe Trail.

But successful windwagons were built. A man named
Wallace, who moved to the town of Washburn in the Texas
Panhandle in 1888, affixed a sail to a spring wagon, devised
a steering system, and made frequent trips to Amarillo and
down through Canyon to Deaf Smith County, tacking the
wagon just like a ship in order to move against the wind.

Perhaps the most successful of the windwagons was
built by Samuel Peppard, who decided that he would travel
by windwagon to the goldfields on Cherry Creek in Kansas
Territory. Originally from Ohio, Peppard had been living
in Oskaloosa for about four years before setting out in May
of 1860, so he knew something of prairie winds. His wagon
had a box eight by three feet and was powered by two sails
mounted on a ten-foot mast. His trip along the Oregon
Trail was exciting, with Indians occasionally racing alongside, amazed at the sight of this early horseless carriage.
The wagon traveled as fast as thirty miles per hour and
in one three-hour, fifty-mile stretch passed 625 wagons
pulled by teams. Peppard left the Oregon Trail near the
site of present-day North Platte, Nebraska, heading southwest toward Denver. A little over a month after leaving
(during which they had favorable winds for only nine days)
and within fifty miles of their goal, the travelers ran afoul
of a dust devil. Their wagon was demolished, ending an
adventurous ride of some five hundred miles.

The most ingenious of these ingenious inventions that
I have learned of (and I would like to learn more) was
made in Plainview, Texas. This particular windwagon dis-

pensed with sails and the accompanying problems of tacking and of whirlwinds by having a windmill built right onto
the wagon bed, a system of gears turning the wagon wheels.
I don't know whether any pictures of this windwagon have
survived, but there do exist some contemporaneous drawings and photographs of sailwagons, monuments to the in-
ventors, many of them anonymous, who attempted to turn
the prairie winds to advantage. Once the oil glut is over
and gasoline prices shoot up again, we could probably use
another Windwagon Smith.—*JH*

98. *The Caboose*

IT'S A SAD DAY in my life. I'd heard it was going to happen,
but somehow I didn't believe it ever would. But it did. I saw
a freight train on the Santa Fe today, a long one—over
eighty cars—and it had no caboose.

According to the railroads, cabooses and the workers
they carry (brakeman and conductor) are no longer necessary for safety. The unions, as I understand it, think that
the caboose and the workers are more reliable than com-
puters and automation in spotting mechanical problems
and preventing accidents. Undoubtedly the elimination of
the caboose and the workers will save money and if safety
really isn't a factor, then why not? Because it's just not a
train without a caboose, that's why not.

It was bad enough when the diesel replaced the steam
engine back in the 1950s. You could be miles from the
tracks, but if you were on high ground you could see the
smoke pouring from the stacks of the old steam engines.
Or if the wind was from the right direction, you could hear
every steam whistle that blew.

What a sound! No wonder the train was such a powerful force in American folk music. Not that the horn—or
hum—of a diesel locomotive isn't a colorful sound. But it
isn't authoritative. I know that at shipping time we had a

little more trouble getting cattle across the tracks and into the Cassoday stockyards without having a train split the herd when diesels replaced the steam engines. You just couldn't hear them coming the way you could a steamer.

One of the joys at shipping time (for us kids, anyway) was going into cabooses and looking around. They were fascinating: benches and tables, lanterns, water coolers, the seats high up in the observation windows, little coal stoves for keeping warm in winter. I never rode in a caboose to the Kansas City stockyards with a load of cattle, but I've known several people who did. That was one of the privileges of the cattle shipper—free passage for himself or one of his hands to accompany the cattle.

In addition to these nostalgic reasons for keeping cabooses, I also have sentimental ones; Grandpa Rice was a brakie on the Missouri Pacific, working his way up to conductor. He spent a lot of time in a caboose, and I loved to hear him talk about the railroad.

What I don't have, I'm afraid, are any logical reasons for keeping cabooses (unless they are indeed a safety factor). And I will admit that the old rule of a caboose for every engine was often carried to absurd lengths—I have seen an engine taking a couple of cars to one of the manufacturing companies a mile or so from the Emporia train yards, caboose attached.

Still, a train without a caboose lacks aesthetic completeness, like a sentence without

See what I mean? Unfortunately, I don't believe the train companies will choose aesthetics over economics.—*JH*

Index of Names